iParenting Media Awards Winner

# What to Do When You're
# Scared &
# Worried

## a guide for kids

# James J. Crist, Ph.D.

**free spirit**
PUBLiSHiNG®

Helping kids
help themselves®
since 1983

**Library of Congress Cataloging-in-Publication Data**
Crist, James J.
    What to do when you're scared & worried : a guide for kids / James J. Crist.
        v. cm.
    Includes bibliographical references and index.
    Contents: Why do we have worries and fears?—Fears after something bad has happened—Fears of people, animals, and situations—Worries about being away from your parents : separation anxiety—Thoughts and behaviors you can't stop—Worrying all the time—Panic, feeling you are going crazy or about to die—How to control your worries and fears—When fears and worries will not go away—For parents : helping your children cope with worries and fears.
        ISBN 1-57542-153-4
    1. Fear—Juvenile literature. 2. Worry—Juvenile literature. [1. Fear. 2. Worry.] I. Title.
        BF575.F2C75 2004
        152.4'6—dc22
                                                                    2003021109

At the time of this book's publication, all facts and figures cited are the most current available. All telephone numbers, addresses, and Web site URLs are accurate and active; all publications, organizations, Web sites, and other resources exist as described in this book; and all have been verified as of February 2007. The author and Free Spirit Publishing make no warranty or guarantee concerning the information and materials given out by organizations or content found at Web sites, and we are not responsible for any changes that occur after this book's publication. If you find an error or believe that a resource listed here is not as described, please contact Free Spirit Publishing. Parents, teachers, and other adults: We strongly urge you to monitor children's use of the Internet.

The concepts, ideas, procedures, and suggestions contained in this book are not intended as a substitute for professional help or therapy.

Edited by Pat Samples and Elizabeth Verdick
Illustrated by Michael Chesworth
Cover and interior design by Marieka Heinlen
Index by Ina Gravitz

10 9 8 7 6
Printed in the United States of America

**Free Spirit Publishing Inc.**
217 Fifth Avenue North, Suite 200
Minneapolis, MN 55401-1299
(612) 338-2068
help4kids@freespirit.com
www.freespirit.com

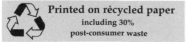

**Printed on recycled paper**
including 30%
post-consumer waste

Free Spirit Publishing is a member of the Green Press Initiative, and we're committed to printing our books on recycled paper containing a minimum of 30% post-consumer waste (PCW). For every ton of books printed on 30% PCW recycled paper, we save 5.1 trees, 2,100 gallons of water, 114 gallons of oil, 18 pounds of air pollution, 1,230 kilowatt hours of energy, and .9 cubic yards of landfill space. At Free Spirit it's our goal to nurture not only young people, but nature too!

green
press
INITIATIVE

# Contents

# Dedication

I dedicate this book to all the young people I have worked with who have struggled with fears and worries. I've learned a lot from watching them, and I hope that other kids will have an easier time as a result.

# Acknowledgments

I would like to thank my editors at Free Spirit, Pat Samples and Elizabeth Verdick, for all their help and revisions. Thank you to my niece, Ariel White, for reviewing the initial manuscript. Finally, I would like to thank my coworkers at the Child and Family Counseling Center for all their encouragement and support.

# Introduction

This book is all about fears and worries—things that everyone deals with at some point in their lives. Whether you're scared and worried some of the time or most of the time, this book can help.

I wrote this book because I'm a psychologist, and I've seen and worked with lots of kids who were scared and worried. Their fears and worries were making their lives more difficult. And no wonder: it can be hard to sleep, eat, think, concentrate, have fun, or get through the day when fears and worries get in the way.

Being scared and worried often leads to feelings of loneliness—but you're *not* alone. And you don't have to try to handle your fears and worries all by yourself. I encourage you to read this book with someone at home who takes care of you: a family grown-up such as a parent or stepparent, a foster parent, a guardian, a grandparent, or an aunt or uncle. The "Note to Grown-ups" on pages 114–119 offers tips for adults who take care

1

of you; be sure to show this special section to your adult helper.

You may also need the guidance of an adult who specializes in treating kids who have problems with their worries and fears: a counselor, psychologist, child psychiatrist, therapist, or doctor, for example. That may seem scary to think about, but experts like these can really help. If you're wondering what it's like to get counseling, see chapter 11.

There are many other people out there who can help you as well. You might talk to your teacher, your principal, your best friend's mom or dad, an adult neighbor you trust, or someone at your place of worship. If you want, you can talk to people your own age, too.

At first, talking about what scares or worries you might feel uncomfortable. Maybe you've kept your fears and worries inside for a long time, and you don't know how to tell anyone about them. The best place to start is with a family grown-up. You might say: "I'm scared and worried about something. Can I talk to you about it?" Just getting those words out can be a big relief.

# Sneak Preview (What's Inside This Book)

Part 1 of *What to Do When You're Scared & Worried* focuses on fears and worries that most kids have.

■ Chapter 1 discusses what other kids are scared and worried about, and what may be bothering you.

■ Chapter 2 looks at where these fears and worries come from, and how the body and mind work together to make fears worse or better.

■ Chapter 3 has ten "Fear Chasers and Worry Erasers," or coping skills you can try at home, at school, or anywhere else.

■ Chapter 4 offers more tools, including some written exercises that can help you get a handle on your fears.

Part 2 focuses on bigger worries and fears—ones that are too hard to handle alone. If you have some of the problems described in chapters 5–10, please talk to a family grown-up right away. You may need the help of a counselor or doctor who can identify your problem and suggest solutions.

■ Chapter 5 talks about specific fears called **Phobias**—fears so strong that they're out of control.

- Chapter 6 discusses the fear of being away from parents or other family grown-ups (it's called **Separation Anxiety**).

- Chapter 7 is about **Generalized Anxiety Disorder,** or constant worrying that occurs for more than six months.

- Chapter 8 has information about **Panic Attacks**—when your heart starts racing and you think you might go crazy, or even die.

- Chapter 9 is about OCD, or **Obsessive-Compulsive Disorder,** which describes being bothered by the same thoughts over and over, or doing the same actions without being able to stop.

- Chapter 10 talks about **Post-Traumatic Stress Disorder,** which affects some people who have experienced or seen horrible events like an accident or violence.

- Chapter 11 describes what it's like to go to counseling. If you're having a very hard time getting over your fears and worries, or if you have problems that are too big to handle on your own, you'll learn how an expert can help.

It may help to know that many kids and adults have overcome their fears by using ideas like the ones in this book, and *you* can, too. It may take some practice, but it will be worth it.

I'd like to know whether this book has helped you and how you're coping with your worries. You can also write to me if you have questions or a problem that you don't know how to handle.

You can email me at:
help4kids@freespirit.com

or send me a letter care of:
Free Spirit Publishing
217 Fifth Avenue North, Suite 200
Minneapolis, MN 55401-1299

Be sure to send me your address, so I can write back to you. I look forward to hearing from you!

# Dr. James J. Crist

# Part 1

## Getting to Know Your Fears and Worries

# Chapter 1

# Kinds of Fears and Worries

**Lupe,** age twelve, worries about not being liked at school. She worries a lot when she's at school, but she can't stop worrying about it even when she's at home. Just thinking about school makes her feel worse.

■ ■ ■

**Salim** is nine, and he's scared about spiders falling on him while he sleeps. He thinks they might be crawling across the ceiling of his bedroom at night, and since it's dark he worries because he can't see them. Salim knows it doesn't help to worry, and he hasn't actually seen any spiders, but he can't stop thinking about them. His worries make it very hard for him to fall asleep.

■ ■ ■

Ten-year-old **Emily** is afraid of thunderstorms. When she sees lightning and hears thunder booming, she runs to her parents. Even her dog gets scared and howls.

7

All kids have worries and fears. Some kids are afraid of one particular thing, like bugs or dogs or storms. And other kids are afraid of lots of stuff—everything from getting lost to being alone. Worries and fears are normal at any age, even for adults.

As people grow older, some of the fears they had as children go away. For example, many young children are scared of the dark. They worry about monsters in the closet and become frightened when the lights get turned off at bedtime. But as these children grow older, many stop being so scared of the dark. Why do people outgrow some of their fears? Because they learn to understand the difference between a real danger and something that won't actually cause harm. They also learn helpful ways to stay safe.

Still, older kids and teenagers worry about many things, such as:

grades

being popular

world problems like poverty, pollution, and war

leaving home

being rejected by other kids

finding a job

death

finding a boyfriend/girlfriend

scary things on TV or close to home, such as crime or violence

Adults worry, too. You may have overheard some of the grown-ups you know worrying about having enough money or making good decisions about the future. Most parents worry a lot about the health and safety of their kids. Often, grown-ups have the same kinds of fears and worries that young people have: being a victim of violence, losing a loved one, or failing in some way, for example.

No matter how old you are, admitting that you're afraid or worried isn't always easy. For one thing, you might feel embarrassed. You may think you should act "tougher" or that you're "too old" to be scared. But it's okay to have worries and fears! If you pretend that your fears and worries don't exist, it's a lot harder to deal with them—especially if they bother you a lot. For another thing, you might not know how to describe what's upsetting you. This is because worries can be difficult to understand, explain, or talk about.

**For example:**

- You may know exactly what you're worried about, such as a bully at school or money problems in your family. But you may not feel comfortable talking about these things. (Talking can help, though. Read more about that in chapter 3.)

- You may feel scared and worried, but not know why. Then it can be hard to put your worries into words.

- You may know what you're scared about (a math test) and, at the same time, realize that worrying about it won't help. But you may worry anyway and end up feeling unable to stop.

Sometimes, you may not realize you're scared and worried until your BODY tells you so. You might get a stomachache or feel tension in your neck and shoulders. You can read more about body "messages" like these in chapter 2.

Worries and fears can be very confusing. The good news is that by noticing and understanding your fears and worries, you can learn to handle them.

# What Scares or Worries You?

Your fears and worries might feel big or small. They might bother you all day long or just some of the time. Either way, this book can help. But first you have to figure out what those fears and worries are.

On pages 12–13 you'll find a list of many common fears among kids. You can use the list to figure out what scares or worries you. Start by photocopying the pages so you don't have to write in the book. If you make several copies, you can fill out the list again and again as your fears and worries change.

For some kids, working on a list of fears and worries feels scary. For other kids, it's scary to look at the finished list and realize how many fears and worries they actually have. If any of this is true for you, be sure to ask your adult helper for support.

# My "Fears and Worries" List

Read the "I'm afraid of" statements first. If you never have that fear, put an X under NO. If you have that fear sometimes, put an X under SOMETIMES. If you have it almost every day, put an X under A LOT.

There are extra lines at the bottom of the list so you can add other fears you have. Once you're done, decide which fear to work on first and circle it. The ideas in chapters 3 and 4 can help you start putting your fears and worries to rest.

| I'm afraid of: | NO | SOMETIMES | A LOT |
|---|---|---|---|
| Thunderstorms | | | |
| Nightmares | | | |
| Getting yelled at | | | |
| Getting into fights | | | |
| Getting laughed at | | | |
| Strangers | | | |
| Doctors or dentists | | | |
| Making mistakes | | | |
| Taking tests | | | |
| Being picked last for a team | | | |
| Not fitting in at school | | | |
| Failing in school | | | |

*continued* ⟶

My *"Fears and Worries" List continued*

| I'm afraid of: | NO | SOMETIMES | A LOT |
|---|---|---|---|
| Wild animals | | | |
| Spiders or bugs | | | |
| Dogs or cats | | | |
| Heights | | | |
| Talking in front of people | | | |
| Meeting new people | | | |
| Enclosed or small spaces | | | |
| Clowns | | | |
| Ghosts or monsters | | | |
| Blood | | | |
| Guns or violence | | | |
| Loud noises | | | |
| Being home alone or away from parents | | | |
| War or terrorism | | | |
| Something bad happening | | | |
| The dark | | | |
| | | | |
| | | | |
| | | | |

It may be helpful to get a journal
or notebook to store your list in, so
you'll always know where to
find it. You can use this same
journal for working on the
ideas in chapter 4, or just
for writing what you're
learning about your worries

and fears. Lots of kids use journals as a place to put
their private thoughts and feelings.

If you like the idea of keeping a journal, here are
other things to write about:

How does it feel when you're scared and worried? What goes on in your mind and body?

Which fears cause you the most trouble, and
why?

Who can you talk to about what's bothering
you? What might you say? How might this
person help?

■ ■ ■

You may find it helpful to ask other people in your
family about their fears and worries. What scares
them? How do they deal with those fears? Talk to
your mom or dad, your brother or sister, a grandparent, or anyone else you trust. If you want, you
can write what you learn in your journal.

# Chapter 2

# Where Do Fears and Worries Come from?

Believe it or not, fears and worries aren't always a bad thing—and they exist for a very good reason. There are times when being scared or worried actually *helps* you.

Think about it this way: if a bully was about to punch you, you'd probably be afraid. That's a *positive* thing because the fear is a form of protection. When you sense danger, your body goes into action. It makes chemicals that get you ready to fight, run away, or stay perfectly still. Experts call this "fight, flight, or freeze."

The reactions in your body happen in just seconds. You can't help it that your body acts this way. In fact, you were born to have this reaction. This is because long ago when the first humans had to protect themselves against wild animals and other dangers, there were basically three ways to stay alive: fight off attackers, run from them, or get very still, trying not to be noticed.

Just like the first humans, people today are programmed for the "fight, flight, or freeze" response. You can think of it as your body's built-in Red Alert. Here's what happens when your body starts producing *adrenaline,* a chemical that boosts your energy:

**Fight Alert:** Your heart pumps more blood so you have the strength to fight. The adrenaline flows through your body, giving you a quick burst of energy.

**Flight Alert:** Your body revs up so you can run faster, and the blood flows to your legs so you can get away. This helps you escape the danger.

**Freeze Alert:** Your body makes you stop in your tracks, so you can't move even if you want to. You still feel revved up, but the energy isn't used for fighting or running.

Adrenaline also causes other temporary changes in your body. You may experience:

■ cold hands and feet; they may get sweaty, too

■ breaking out in a sweat all over

- butterflies in your stomach, or a stomachache

- feeling like you can't think straight

- a rush of blood to your face and scalp (maybe your hair even "stands on end")

- goose bumps or goose pimples (that's when the hair on your body bristles, making the skin around it appear bumpy)

It's normal to have all these reactions. They go away when the adrenaline stops flowing.

Your brain plays a big role in all of these body changes. That's because your brain has a fear center known as the *amygdala*. You might think of it as your brain's guard post that helps keep you safe. When your eyes or ears sense any kind of danger, your brain gets the message. The amygdala then checks with your brain's memory to see if the sight or sound matches what you know to be dangerous. If a threat exists, your Red Alert system turns on.

There *are* times when running to safety is the right thing to do. If you're being bullied or if you see someone with a gun, you need to get yourself to safety—and quick. But what about fighting? Fighting isn't a solution. Getting aggressive or trying to hurt someone will only make things worse for you. This is why it's so important to understand "fight, flight, or freeze" and what you can do when it happens to you.

Once this happens, you go on "automatic." You react by instinct, which means you react almost without thinking. There's usually little or no time to figure out whether you really need to be afraid or not.

Today, you may not be in great danger of an attack by a wild animal, but your body still reacts as if you are. When you feel threatened, your body gets pumped up to fight, flee, or freeze. This reaction happens whether the "danger" is a quiz at school, a visit to the dentist, or a performance in front of an audience. The problem is that your body's automatic way of reacting doesn't help in these situations. It's not to your advantage to run away from your quiz, punch your dentist, or freeze when you're onstage!

# Your Thoughts and Feelings Are Connected

Even though your body has a built-in fear response, you *do* have some control over your next move. Your automatic response may be to fight, run, or freeze up—but you don't always have to do one of those things. Remember that your amygdala wants to protect you from harm. So, changing how you *think* about a particular danger is a clever way of telling your brain and body to react differently.

Here's an example: Suppose you have a fear of blood, and you can't even look if someone gets a small cut. The sight of blood might make you feel sick, dizzy, or freaked out. If so, your automatic reaction may be to run away and hide.

But what if you were to change how you think about blood? First, ask yourself *why* you're afraid of it. If your brain tells you something like, "Bleeding means you're going to die," of course you'll be scared! But what if you were to change that thought to, "Bleeding is the body's way of cleaning out a cut and repairing itself"? That knowledge—that *thought*—could begin to calm you down. Now you're using the thinking part of your brain to handle your fears.

You don't even have to be in a scary situation for your body to react. You can just be playing a video game or watching something scary on TV, and your body will still react as if you were in real danger—usually by freezing up. Have you ever noticed that your muscles get tense when you're playing video games? Or that your heart races and you start breathing faster as you watch a scary movie? You can thank your "fight, flight, or freeze" response for that!

To handle your worries and fears, you need to remember that these feelings are sending you a message. You can listen to your feelings, figure out what you're afraid of and why, and then decide what to do.

## Jamal's Story

Twelve-year-old Jamal was afraid to go to school because other kids teased him in the halls and during class. They picked on Jamal because he had trouble learning. Jamal was so afraid of being teased that he got stomachaches and headaches every morning. The aches and pains were telling him he was scared and worried.

Some mornings, Jamal's head and stomach hurt so much that he stayed home. But that didn't solve his problem, because he still had to face those kids when he went back to school. He knew he needed to learn how to handle the teasing so he could stop feeling sick.

Jamal decided to talk to his teacher about it. She suggested that Jamal try an experiment for a few days: whenever the kids teased him, Jamal would imagine them wearing really goofy clothes. The purpose of the experiment was to help Jamal laugh instead of getting upset when he was teased.

Jamal's strategy worked because he was *changing his thoughts* about the teasing. Instead of believing what the other kids said, he focused on laughing it off. He no longer felt so tense, and because the other kids didn't know why he was laughing, they decided to leave Jamal alone. Within a few days, Jamal started to feel more confident. As his anxiety gradually faded, his aches and pains started to go away, too.

Sometimes, thinking about a fear or worry in a new way can help you find solutions. For example, do you get scared when you have to talk in front of the class or get up in front of an audience? If so, it's normal for your heart to start racing or for your stomach to hurt. Instead of seeing this physical reaction as a problem, think of it as your body's way of getting excited. Make use of that extra energy by trying your hardest to do your best. It may also help to take a few deep breaths to calm yourself down. See what works for *you*.

■ ■ ■

The better you get at figuring out new ways of handling your worries and fears, the less often your Red Alert response will be triggered. And when it *is* triggered, you'll know better what to do.

Chapter 3 has more information about changing your thoughts so you'll feel less worried and afraid. See strategy #2, "Flip the Switch from Negative to Positive," on page 25–26.

# Chapter 3

# Fear Chasers
# and Worry Erasers

Just for a moment, imagine you're a star basketball player about to make the game-winning shot; or pretend you're a famous actor who's about to go onstage to accept an important award. Close your eyes and pay attention to the messages your body is sending. This is your moment of glory and everyone is watching—how do you feel?

Even though it's all imaginary, you might notice a faster heartbeat, get butterflies in your stomach, or feel the excitement rising. Your brain is a very powerful thing. Just *thinking* about an event like this can rev you up.

To take this further, think about what you as a star athlete or an award-winning actor might tell yourself during that big moment. Suppose you were to approach the net or the stage saying, "You're going to make a fool of yourself!" or "Don't blow it now, you big idiot!" What would the result be? You'd feel even more worried. That "fight, flight, or freeze" response (see chapter 2) would go into overdrive, making it harder to score that winning basket or give a great speech.

But what might happen if you were to tell your-self something *positive* like, "Wow, this is my big chance!" or "I can do it, and I'm going to give it my best!" You'd be much more likely to succeed. Athletes, actors, and other people who need to per-form at their best have learned something that the rest of us can learn: how to overcome their fear. If they can do it, so can you.

## Using Fear Chasers and Worry Erasers

Where do you begin? It starts inside your head—with your thoughts. How you *think about* your fears matters a lot. And that's what this chapter is all about.

Here are ten **"Fear Chasers and Worry Erasers"**— strategies you can use when you're scared and wor-ried. The strategies are numbered, but you don't have to use them in any order. You can try just one or two, or do every single one. They're all designed to work together to help you become stronger and calmer.

Although you can use the Fear Chasers and Worry Erasers on your own, they're even more help-ful when a family grown-up is involved. This per-son can be your supporter and can cheer you on whenever you need a boost.

## #1: "Get Real" About Your Fears and Worries

A note about the Fear Chasers and Worry Erasers: the more you practice them, the easier it will be to use them when you need them most. Be sure to have fun with each skill, because the more fun you have, the more you'll want to practice—and that means better results!

Have you been pretending that your fears and worries don't exist? Or ignoring them, hoping they'll go away? Maybe you've tried to act tough, like things aren't really bothering you.

Lots of kids try to hide their worries, or act tough on the outside when they feel scared on the inside. And lots of kids blame themselves for feeling scared. They think, "It's my fault I'm so scared of everything," or "If only I would have done things differently before, I wouldn't be afraid now." But you didn't cause your fears, and blaming yourself won't help.

What *does* help? Admitting that you have fears and worries, just like other people do. It may help to write about what's bothering you. Just putting those fears and worries on paper is a good way to get them out in the open. Once you start being honest with yourself about your fears, it's easier to be honest with other people. You can talk to your family and friends about what's bothering you, and let them help.

Here are some ideas for getting the words out:

- "I feel so worried right now, and I need to talk about it."

- "Sometimes I feel scared and alone. Can you help me?"

- "I've been writing about my feelings in my journal, and I'm learning stuff about myself. Can we talk about my feelings?"

- "Mom, do you worry about stuff a lot? I do, and I was wondering if you do, too."

- "Dad, this is hard for me to talk about, but I'm scared of something and I wanted to tell you about it."

- "Sometimes I just don't understand my feelings. It's hard to put them into words, but I want to talk about them."

- "I've been working on a list of my worries and fears. This is what I came up with. Will you look at it with me, please, and help me out?"

## #2: Flip the Switch from Negative to Positive

Remember that example about the basketball star and the award-winning actor? (See page 22.) Many athletes and celebrities have learned to handle their moments in the spotlight. But those strategies aren't only for the rich and famous! They're useful for anyone who wants to overcome their fears.

Start by learning to switch your thoughts from negative to positive. When you notice yourself thinking negative thoughts like, "I'm going to fail," you can tell yourself to stop. It may help to picture a stop sign in your head or imagine yourself yelling, "Stop!" Immediately replace the bad thought with a good one instead, like this: "I'm going to try hard," or, "I can do it!"

When you turn the switch from negative to positive, your body reacts. You start to feel calmer and stronger. Although you may still have a few butterflies in your stomach or sweaty palms, you'll be able to think a little more clearly. Tell yourself, "I can handle it," and you'll start to feel more confident.

This strategy works not only when you're in a situation that feels scary but at other times, too. Positive thinking can help you every day. That's because when you believe that the best (or something good) will happen, your mood improves.

## Maria's Story

Ten-year-old Maria loved her weekly dance class. But when the teacher said there was going to be a dance recital where all the classes would perform onstage, Maria got scared. Dancing in a small class was one thing; performing in front of a whole bunch of kids and parents was another. She told her dad that she wanted to quit dance forever.

When her dad found out about the recital, he understood that Maria was scared and worried about performing in front of a crowd. But he wanted her to stick with dance. The teacher said Maria could stay in the class but not perform in the recital, so that's what they all agreed on.

During the next few months, Maria learned her dance steps and started to feel more confident; she still had stage fright, though. After class one evening, Maria's teacher pulled her aside to talk. She said lots of dancers were nervous about performances; she also said it might help to focus on the good feelings, instead of the fear. Then her teacher asked, "What's the worst that could happen?" Maria went home to think about that. She and her dad decided to write it all down. The list looked like this:

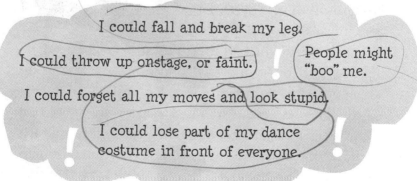

I could fall and break my leg!

I could throw up onstage, or faint.

People might "boo" me.

I could forget all my moves and look stupid.

I could lose part of my dance costume in front of everyone.

"So," her dad asked, "What are the chances of those things happening?" Maria thought about it and decided it wasn't likely that *all* those things would happen. After her next class, she asked her teacher if dancers ever made mistakes at the recital. Her teacher told her that many times she herself forgot a move onstage or did the wrong step. No one booed, though, and most people hardly noticed!

As the day of the recital approached, Maria's dad asked her to concentrate on the *best* that could happen. Maria felt more confident, and she realized all those rehearsals had been worth it. She decided to perform in the recital along with the rest of the class—and enjoy it as much as she could.

If you're scared and worried about something, ask yourself, "What's the worst that could happen?" Usually, the worst isn't as bad as you might think. Your worries might be based on beliefs that aren't true, like: "I'll be a total failure, and everyone will know it," or, "Nothing ever turns out right for me."

Beliefs like these make it harder to overcome your fears. Sure, it's possible that you might make a mistake, but mistakes happen to everyone. You can learn from a mistake and do better next time.

Replace those negative thoughts with positive ones by thinking about the *best* that might happen. That's a smart step toward overcoming your fears.

## #3: Get Your Mind off Your Worries

Sometimes, you can help yourself by taking a break from your worries and fears, and focusing on something else. Suppose you have a spelling test coming up and you're scared you might do poorly on it. Thoughts like these might keep running through your mind:

"I'm going to fail.

This test is going to be impossible!

I don't know how to spell any of the words on my list.

Everyone is going to do better than me.

I never get a good score on my tests.

I just know it's going to be really hard!

Oh, no! My test is in two days!

I can't study because I'm too freaked out."

If your mind starts to get carried away like this, it helps to use idea #2, or "Flip the Switch from Negative to Positive." But you can also give your mind and body a break by doing something fun. Take a bike ride, visit a friend, or read a book—do anything that takes your mind off your worries.

Counting can take your mind off your worries, too. Count slowly to 50 or 100—or higher, if you'd like. As you count, you can picture objects in your mind: sheep jumping over a fence, for example. If you're feeling really scared or worried, count things that make you laugh.

Or, try something that makes you laugh—because it's hard to be scared and laugh at the same time! Get a joke book, read the comics, rent a funny video, or watch a comedy show on TV. Making someone else laugh is another fun way to give your mind a break.

Throughout the day, take time to quiet your mind. For example, go out and explore your backyard or take a walk in your neighborhood. Enjoy a long, hot bath. Writing in your journal is another way to feel more quiet and peaceful.

## #4: Get Active

It's natural to feel revved up when you're scared and worried. That's your body's way of getting ready to protect you from what it thinks might cause you harm. So when the adrenaline kicks in, you may feel like running or fighting—after all, that's what your body is designed to do. But in most situations, it's not really an option to fight or flee. What good are your fists when you're revved up about your math test? And what good would it do to run away when your teacher says it's your turn to give your oral report?

Exercise is a healthy way of using your adrenaline or extra energy. When you exercise, your body uses up the adrenaline and releases chemicals that calm you down. In a way, physical activity "tricks" your body into thinking that the danger has passed. Your body calms down and your worries begin to fade.

Getting active can help you in different ways. First, it can be a release when you're dealing with a situation that feels scary. Suppose you're frightened of going to the doctor, but you know you have no choice about it. Instead of letting yourself worry all day, you could do something active—such as run around on the playground, practice your skateboarding tricks, or go for a jog. You'll not only work your body but you'll also clear your mind.

Exercise helps in another important way, too. When you exercise on a regular basis (every day or several times each week), you have a reliable way of releasing your extra energy. Your heart, lungs, and muscles will get stronger and you'll feel calmer. You'll even sleep better, too. That's an extra bonus if you're scared of the dark or if you have nightmares.

## #5: Be Aware of What You Eat

Eating a healthy, balanced diet—one that includes plenty of fruits and vegetables—is really important at your age. You still have a lot of growing to do, and your bones, muscles, and organs need to be nourished. You get that nourishment from healthy foods that have lots of vitamins and minerals.

A balanced diet helps you feel stronger and more energetic—something that's even more important when you're dealing with fears and worries. Worrying all the time makes your brain feel worn out. And being scared and anxious makes your body feel worn down. At times like that, you need more strength and energy. That's where healthy foods come in.

People who feel scared and worried tend to do three not-so-helpful things: (1) skip meals because they feel too upset to eat, (2) overeat because they use food to get their mind off their worries, and (3) reach for the junk food or caffeine because they think it might help them feel better.

Eating too little or too much isn't healthy. The key to a healthy diet is *balance.* You need nutritious meals and snacks throughout the day, even when your stomach hurts because of your worries. Junk foods like chips, donuts, and candy aren't healthy so try to avoid snacking on them too often. It's okay to eat them once in a while, though. If you have questions about eating right, talk to a family grown-up or ask your doctor, teacher, or school nurse for information.

Have you heard of a "sugar buzz" or a "caffeine buzz"? Sugar makes you feel hyper for a while, and then super tired. Sodas, coffee, and teas that have caffeine in them will give you a burst of adrenaline. (Just like being scared or worried!) But when the caffeine wears off, you'll feel wiped out. To avoid these highs and lows, cut back on caffeine and sugar.

## #6: Practice Deep Breathing and Visualization

Breathing deeply—all the way into your belly—is relaxing. It helps oxygen get to your brain and muscles, which helps them work better and calms you down.

When you're nervous, you may breathe too quickly. You only fill up the top part of your lungs and don't take in enough air. Breathing this way can leave you feeling even more jittery.

It may be hard to believe that you need to learn to breathe right, but many people don't know how!

They take light, shallow breaths—the kind that only fill the top part of the lungs. Look down for a moment and watch your stomach: it should move out and in as you breathe. If it does, that's a sign that you're taking deep breaths. If not, you can learn to breathe deeply, using these instructions:

1.  Place one hand on your stomach.

2.  Breathe in slowly and deeply through your nose. Count to five as you breathe in, and again as you breathe out. Counting like this will help you breathe slowly and deeply.

3.  When you breathe in, try to fill the bottom of your lungs, near your stomach. If you're having trouble doing this, put your hand on your stomach. Then, as you breathe in, let your stomach push out a little. (You should see it moving in and out as you breathe; if you're lying down, you'll see your stomach go up and down.)

4.  After your lungs are full, breathe out slowly. Pretend that as you push the air out of your lungs, your worries are going out with it. Imagine that your worries and fears are like steam that you can see leaving your body.

5.  Repeat these steps over and over—ten times in all. If you still feel anxious, try another ten breaths.

Use deep breathing at home, at school, in the car, on the bus, or anytime you feel nervous. It works great if you have trouble falling asleep at night, too. And now that you know how to breathe deeply, you can use *visualization:* a tool for focusing your thoughts on something positive and peaceful. Visualization can even help with headaches and other pain.

To visualize, close your eyes and take a few deep breaths. When you're ready, think of a happy, peaceful place—real or imaginary. Picture it in your mind as if you're there now. It might help to pretend that you're playing a video of the place in your mind. Pay attention to the sights, the sounds, and the feel of the place.

*For example, picture yourself in a quiet forest; imagine the sound of the wind in the trees and feel the sunshine on your skin.*

You can also imagine being somewhere exciting: an amusement park, body surfing in the ocean, or on the back of a horse as you ride on a trail. While this image might not be relaxing, it can take your mind off your worries.

If you have trouble making up your own image, try one of the following suggestions. Read each idea first and then imagine being in the scene. Or make a tape or CD of each one by reading it aloud and recording it. Play back the recording as you relax and visualize.

- **Snowman:** Imagine you're a snowman, standing alone in the morning sun. As the day heats up, you feel yourself melting bit by bit. First your head starts to melt and then your body, slowly and gradually—drip, drip, drip. As you melt, you feel warmer and more relaxed.

- **Cloud:** Picture yourself on a fluffy white cloud that feels like the softest bed in the  world. As you float by in the big blue sky, your worries drift away in the wind, one by one. Watch them disappear into the blue.

- **Ocean:** Visualize the deep blue ocean. You are a wave in the rolling sea, gently moving up and down. Feel the motion; let it relax you. Hear the sound of the waves in your mind and imagine that they are carrying your worries away.

## #7: Relax Those Muscles

Ever notice how your muscles tense up when you're nervous, worried, or scared? This muscle tension can leave you feeling even more anxious. By relaxing your muscles one group at a time, you'll release some of the tension.

Muscle relaxation is something you can do every day—just like exercise—to help you feel calmer. It works when you're standing up or sitting down, but you may find that it works best when you're lying down.

Start by concentrating on each muscle you're about to relax. For each one, tighten it as hard as you can for one or two seconds, and then release. You can go from head to toe, or in the opposite direction. (In other words, begin with your head and neck, and move down toward your feet; or start at your feet and move up to your legs, stomach, chest, hands, and so on.)

You can do deep breathing (see #6, "Practice Deep Breathing and Visualization," on page 33–36) as you relax your muscles. Once you're relaxed, keep your eyes closed and try some visualization.

## #8: Write About Your Feelings

Keeping a journal has many benefits. When you write about your feelings, you get a chance to understand them better. Thoughts and feelings you

didn't even know you had may start coming out on the paper. You might think, "Wow, I never knew I felt that way."

As you work on different Fear Chasers and Worry Erasers, take notes about them in your journal. What did you learn about yourself? How did the strategy work for you? Here are some other journaling ideas:

Keep a record of how often you exercise, and which activities you enjoy most.

Write about how you're taking care of your body. Are you eating right and avoiding too much junk food and caffeine? Is it helping?

Make a list of things that help you relax.

Write about your grown-up helper and how that person is supporting you.

List positive things you can tell yourself when you're scared and worried.

## #9: Be Aware of Your "Red Alerts"

In chapter 1, there's an exercise called My "Fears and Worries" List (pages 12–13). If you filled out that list, you already know what scares you.

If you haven't filled out that list, you might want to do so now. Chapter 2 talked about your body's built-in Red Alert (pages 16–17), a physical response that gets your body ready to take action.

So, this means you've got a few Red Alert tools to use. You not only have a list of your fears and worries, but you also have information about the signals your body sends when you're scared. Now that you know more about your Red Alerts, you can figure out ways to avoid them or face them, depending on what's right for you.

Suppose you have a fear of loud noises or bugs. You know these things bother you, and you know your Red Alert will turn on when you see or hear them. What can you do? You can avoid concerts or sporting events if you hate loud noises. You can put on bug spray when you're outdoors and make sure you're wearing long sleeves so it's less likely that an insect will touch your skin. In these ways, you can avoid what scares and worries you.

But it's not always possible to avoid things you fear. Suppose you're afraid of the dark or night-mares—or you're scared of meeting new people and not fitting in at school. Your Red Alerts are unavoidable because night always comes, and you have no choice but to sleep; plus, you *have* to go to school. This is where all the strategies in this chapter come in handy. Use the following examples to help you figure out how to put your own Fear Chasers and Worry Erasers to work.

**If you're scared of . . .**

- **the dark or nightmares:** try to relax before bed by doing some deep breathing, visualizing a peaceful place, and using muscle relaxation. Avoid drinking caffeine or eating spicy foods before going to bed. Be sure not to watch scary TV shows or movies at night.

- **bullies, teasing, and not fitting in at school:** build your confidence by making at least one new friend you can spend time with at school—someone who helps you to stick up for yourself if you're teased. Remember to think positive by telling yourself, "I can handle it," for example, or "I am a confident person." Report a bully problem to a teacher or your principal so you don't have to face a bully alone.

- **bad grades, tests, or failing:** talk to a family grown-up or your teacher so you can get more confident about your skills. An adult can help you identify whether you have a learning difficulty or whether you're worrying so much about making mistakes that it's hard for you to focus.

Part 2 contains lots of information on other types of fears and what to do about them. See chapters 5–10 for more on fears and worries that you can't control, even if you try.

■ **violence, war, and terrorism:** realize that everyone is scared of these things, and know that you're definitely not alone. Talking to a grownup can really help, because it's important for you to learn ways to quiet your mind and keep yourself safe.

Remember that no matter what your particular fears are, you can make an effort to handle them. When they start to bother you, try doing something physical so you can burn off the extra energy. If it's not possible to exercise, see if deep breathing helps. Be sure to work on your *thoughts* by telling yourself something positive and calming. Talk to someone else, if possible, or write in your journal. You may need to try a combination of ideas until you start feeling better.

Here's another way of getting a grip on your Red Alerts. Try repeating what you're afraid of 50, 100, or even 500 times. You can do this in your mind, or you can write the fears out on paper. Why does this work? Usually, most kids try to *avoid* thinking about what they're worried about, to get it out of their mind. But by repeating the fear over and over, your mind gets used to the thought. Suppose you spend time thinking, "I'm afraid of storms, I'm afraid of storms," and then you write it down 50 times. You may notice that the words no longer feel as scary. (Experts call this *desensitizing*.) Another option is to say the words in your head or out loud using a silly voice, which can help change the way you think about your fear. Try it and see.

## #10: Tell Others What You've Learned

Some of the people around you may not understand your worries and fears, and may say things like, "You're always such a wreck," or, "Why don't you lighten up?" While it may hurt or anger you to hear such things, you can respond in a way that helps the other person understand you better:

- Explain that your brain sometimes is too quick to think that something is scary or dangerous.

- Say that you have to work harder than most kids at overcoming your fears.

- Mention that your amygdala switches on too quickly! To explain what you mean, you can tell the person about how the amygdala acts like a guard post and is only trying to keep you safe.

- Remind that person, "Everyone has things they're scared of and worried about, and it's not like you have to hide it."

■ ■ ■

Talk to your friends and family about the Fear Chasers and Worry Erasers, and ask people to support you as you try the strategies. Show your supporters how to do fun things like deep breathing or visualization. Your family and friends might even want to try these activities with you.

## Chapter 4

# Going Further:
# Pencil and Paper Exercises

For some kids, using the Fear Chasers and Worry Erasers from chapter 3 is enough to handle what's bothering them. But others may need (or want) to go a bit further. In this chapter, you'll find pencil and paper exercises that have been helpful for the kids I've worked with. You can try these written activities yourself and see if they work for you, too.

If you don't have one already, it's time to get an adult helper: someone you trust who can look over the exercises with you and show you what to do. The written exercises may stir up emotions that are difficult to handle alone. Dealing with these feelings will be easier if you have an adult to guide and support you. If it isn't possible for a family grown-up to help, ask your teacher or your school counselor.

If at any time you realize that working on these exercises makes you feel *more* worried, then stop and take a break for as long as you need. Talk about your feelings with an adult you trust. When you're ready, you can begin again.

# Start with Your Journal

If you've already tried the journaling ideas on pages 14 and 37–38, that's great. You can use the same journal for all of the exercises in chapter 4. If you don't have a journal already, now is a good time to start one. If you choose not to use a journal, a pencil and paper will work, too.

Before starting the written exercises below, it's recommended that you review the My "Fears and Worries" List from chapter 1 (see pages 12–13). Decide which fear or worry is giving you the most trouble, and then focus on that one as you read chapter 4.

## Write Your Goal

Set a positive goal for handling your fear. To do this, first decide what you want to achieve, and then word your goal in a way that will help you to succeed. Your goal should state positively what you "will" be able to do.

### Examples of goals:

 I will make at least one new friend this month.

 I will be able to stay home alone for at least one hour.

I will be able to go outside and not be afraid of bugs.

Putting your goal on a paper is a great way to see it clearly and get excited about it. Keep this written goal in your journal and someplace else where you can see it every day: on your mirror, in your locker, or on a bulletin board at home. Look at your goal often, and practice saying it out loud. Remind yourself to think positive, as in, "I can do it!"

You can also try this goal-related exercise in your journal:

1. **Draw a picture of what you're most afraid of**—this can be an object, such as the classroom pet, or a situation, such as speaking up in class.

2. **Now draw a second picture. This time, draw the worst possible thing you can imagine happening, as it relates to your fear.** For example, you might draw the classroom pet biting your finger, or draw the kids in your class throwing rotten apples at you while you talk. If this feels too scary or makes you feel worse, you can skip to Step 3.

3.  **Finally, draw a picture of you handling your fear successfully.** Make this drawing as positive as possible. (Show yourself holding the class pet with a big smile on your face or talking in class while everyone listens happily.) Put this picture where you can see it—on your bedroom wall or on the cover of your journal. Every day, look at the picture and tell yourself that *this* is your goal—the very thing you *will* make happen.

## List Good Reasons Not to Be Afraid

Here's another positive way to write about your fear: list several reasons *not* to be afraid. Make sure these reasons are *positive*. So, you don't want to include reasons such as, "I'm stupid for being afraid," or, "No one else is worried about this but me."

Here's an example of how to word things positively. Ten-year-old Dustin was avoiding the playground because he had been bullied there a few months earlier. He decided he was ready to get out there and have fun on the playground again, so he made that his goal. Then he listed five reasons not to be afraid:

## Good Reasons Not to Be Afraid to Go Back on the Playground

1. The kid that hurt me got in trouble for what he did.

2. My friends will be with me to protect me.

3. I will yell, run, or get an adult if he tries again.

4. I told my guidance counselor and my teacher about my fear, and the adults at school are looking out for me.

5. The playground is for everyone—and that means I get to be there, too.

Try to come up with at least three good reasons—the more the better. Next, read your reasons aloud or ask your grown-up helper to read them to you. Hearing the words spoken can help them sink in.

# Make a Fear Scale

This exercise is called a Fear Scale, because it's a way of "ranking" the thoughts and actions that relate to your fear. Here's how it works: First, you make a list of every action you can think of that's connected to your fear. If you're afraid of dogs (as in the next example), you might list how you feel when you see, hear, touch, or simply think of dogs.

Next, you rank each of the items on your list, using a scale of numbers from 0 to 100. First, give the fear a number that tells you how anxious you feel about it; the higher the number, the more anxious you are. In the example below, 100 is the highest number. After that, you can rank the items on your list, in order. Put the fear with the highest number on top and the one with the lowest at the bottom.

Eleven-year-old Diego was afraid of dogs. His Fear Scale looked like this:

| THINGS RELATED TO MY FEAR OF DOGS | HOW SCARY? 0 (just a little scary) –100 (very scary) |
|---|---|
| giving a dog a bone | 90 |
| petting a dog | 80 |
| walking toward a strange dog | 70 |
| walking past a dog on a leash | 60 |
| seeing a dog behind a fence barking at me | 50 |
| hearing a dog bark | 30 |
| thinking about dogs | 10 |
| looking outside and seeing a dog walk by | 10 |

Once you've made your own list, the next step is to *think about* each item on your Fear Scale. As you imagine each item, your Red Alert (see pages 16–18) will most likely go on. Your goal here is to calm down, relax, and start to think about each item on your list again with *confidence* instead of fear.

**ALERT!**

You can take deep breaths and try to relax your muscles. Imagine yourself in a safe and peaceful place. Once you're relaxed, you're ready to begin working your way up your Fear Scale. *Start at the bottom*, with the fear that has the lowest number. Close your eyes and imagine that you're doing the activity that goes along with that number.

For example, Diego started thinking about a dog by picturing one in his mind. As his Red Alert went on, he focused on calming down. He practiced thinking about the dog until he could do so calmly (it took several tries). Diego continued with his Fear Scale, practicing each item on the list. He saw himself watching a dog go by, hearing it bark, and eventually petting the dog. Each time he became too anxious, he took several deep breaths and tried to relax again. By going through this entire exercise slowly, Diego was able to think about each item on his Fear Scale until he could do so without feeling afraid.

You can do the same thing with your own Fear Scale. Go through each step on it, staying as relaxed as you can. Once you've completed a step, go to the next highest fear on your list. Remember, it can take days or weeks to go through your Fear Scale. You may have to do this exercise *many times* until you're ready to go up to the next item on your scale.

If you get anxious anytime while you're working your way up the Fear Scale, stop and relax again, as you did before you started. Rate how afraid you feel at the moment—this time using a scale of 0–10, with 10 being extremely afraid and 0 being not afraid at all. When your worry drops to at least a 3 or so, or to a point at which you can imagine the activity without feeling too afraid, you are ready to move on. Continue until your feelings of fear are gone, or almost gone. If you have trouble relaxing, you can try thinking of something funny and see if that helps you calm down.

This exercise works best if you practice it *every day*. Once you can imagine the scariest part of your fear without feeling too worried, you're ready for the next BIG step—facing your fear head-on (keep reading).

# Face Your Fear

To face your fear, use the same list that you created for your Fear Scale above. This time, instead of just *imagining* each step, you'll actually *try* it. Start with the easiest item on the list, the one that appears at the bottom. (Using the example on page 48, Diego's first step was looking outside and seeing a dog go by.) Be sure to ask a family grown-up to stay with you as you take the first step on your own Fear Scale.

Once you're able to take that step without feeling so afraid, you're ready to go on to the next one, and the next one after that. It may take several days or weeks of doing each step before you're ready for the next one on your Fear Scale—that's okay! Take all the time you need. If you get too anxious, take a break. Once you have calmed down or when you feel ready, start again.

Facing your fear will be scary at first, and that's totally normal. Remind yourself to keep your eye on your goal (the one you wrote down in your journal). As you continue facing this fear, it may help to use some of the Fear Chasers and Worry Erasers from chapter 3—things like deep breathing, muscle relaxation, exercise, and positive thinking. Keep at it and don't give up.

Tameka, age thirteen, used a Fear Scale for her worries. After she was in a car accident, she was afraid of riding in a car again and she worried about it all the time. She decided to set a goal of not only riding in a car again but also going past the place where the accident happened. This was her Fear Scale:

| THINGS RELATED TO MY FEAR OF RIDING IN CARS | HOW SCARY? 0 (just a little scary) – 100 (very scary) |
|---|---|
| driving past the place where the accident happened | 100 |
| stopping at a stoplight or stop sign | 95 |
| the car starts moving | 90 |
| Mom or Dad starting the car | 80 |
| buckling my seat belt | 70 |
| getting in the car | 50 |
| opening the car door | 40 |
| walking out of the house | 20 |
| getting ready to go for a car ride | 10 |

Tameka's list of reasons not to be scared and worried:

## Good Reasons Not to Be Afraid to Ride in Cars

1. Mom is a very good driver, and so is Dad.

2. They will slow down if I ask them to.

3. Accidents do not happen often.

4. My seat belt will help keep me safe.

Tameka followed the steps on her Fear Scale, first in her imagination and then for real. Each time she felt her stomach getting tense, she stopped and relaxed again. This wasn't a quick or easy process for her—but it worked. Eventually, Tameka could ride in a car again and she was able to visit the scene of the accident. That was a scary thing to do, but afterward, she felt much more confident and better able to handle her fears.

■ ■ ■

Getting rid of a fear takes time and practice. Try to practice every day—for as long as you can. The more time you spend practicing, the faster your fear will go away. And that's worth the effort!

# Part 2

## Getting Help for Hard-to-Handle Problems

## Chapter 5

# When Fears Are Out of Control

## (Phobias)

Most kids get over a lot of their fears as they get older because they learn that what they're afraid of isn't really dangerous, or they learn how to protect themselves from the danger. But what about fears that don't go away over time?

When people keep being bothered by their fear, or they can't even go outside or have fun because of it, the fear may have become a phobia. A phobia is a fear so strong that it's out of control. People can develop phobias about almost anything— animals, other people, heights, thunderstorms, or the sight of blood.

How do you know if you have a phobia? Ask yourself if your fear keeps you from doing things you really *want* or *need* to do. Is your fear so strong that it's controlling your life?

■ ■ ■

For example, thirteen-year-old Maya was so afraid of cats that she wouldn't go outside. She wanted to play with her friends, but she stayed indoors because she was scared that a cat would be there.

Eleven-year-old **Devon** was so scared of being in a crowd of people that he wouldn't go to the mall with his friends, even though he thought it would be fun. Both Devon and Maya had phobias. Just *thinking* about what they were afraid of stopped them from doing the things they wanted to do.

■ ■ ■

The *power* of the scared feelings is the clue that a fear has become a phobia. The fear feels *huge*, and it comes up every time you think about the thing you  fear or if you're around it. Your heart starts pounding, your muscles tense up, and you may even feel dizzy— that's your Red Alert turning on. (See chapter 2 for more about the Red Alert.) You may start sweating, get an upset stomach, and feel shaky, too.

ALERT!

If you have a phobia, it's probably getting in the way of your usual activities. You may be afraid to go places with your friends because you think you might run into something you fear. Friends may eventually stop calling you because you never want to go to the park, the movies, the mall, or to somebody else's home. You might know that you don't need to be so afraid, but this doesn't make

Only a doctor or therapist can say for sure if you have a phobia. That's why it's so important to talk to an adult and get some expert help.

the fear go away. If other kids and adults don't understand why you're so afraid, the situation can be even more difficult for you.

# Phobias have their own fancy names:

| A fear of: | is known as: |
| --- | --- |
| animals | zoophobia |
| anything new | neophobia |
| being trapped in small spaces | claustrophobia |
| blood | hematophobia |
| cats | gatophobia or ailurophobia |
| death | thanatophobia |
| dogs | cynophobia |
| ghosts | phasmophobia |
| insects | entomophobia |
| heights | acrophobia |
| open spaces or going outside of your home | agoraphobia |
| snakes | ophidophobia |
| spiders | arachnophobia |
| water | hydrophobia |

No one knows for sure why some kids have phobias while others don't. Some fears seem to be inherited, which means that if your dad, mom, or other relatives have phobias, you're more likely to have one yourself. Sometimes a phobia develops after a bad experience. If you were bitten badly by a cat when you were younger, for example, you might develop a phobia based on a fear that *all* cats will bite you—even though it's not likely to happen.

How does a fear become a phobia? As you learned in chapter 2, your *amygdala* (see page 17) switches on when it senses danger. But your amygdala can't always tell the difference between things you really *do* need to be afraid of and things that won't cause you harm. When you have a phobia, your brain turns on the fear switch and you can't get it to turn off no matter how hard you try.

## Social Phobia

One of the most common phobias among kids is called *social phobia*—a fear of other people and social situations. (Another name for this fear is *social anxiety disorder.*) This phobia isn't the same as shyness. Kids who have social phobia have a fear so intense that it's hard for them to join a team, go to parties or to camp, go to school, or meet new people.

## Andrea's Story

Thirteen-year-old Andrea was so afraid to meet new people that she had very few friends. When other people talked to her, she looked the other way because she was afraid to look people in the eye. She was terrified that she would say something silly or embarrassing, or that someone would make fun of her. Other kids thought Andrea was a snob or that she didn't like them because she hardly ever talked to anyone.

Andrea was too afraid to speak up, even though she wanted friends. She hated being in a group of people because she didn't feel that she could talk without everyone staring at her. Any time she tried to be social, she got so afraid that her heart raced, her mouth and throat got dry, and she started to shake. This reaction was too hard for her to take, so she ended up walking away, feeling sad and lonely. She was even afraid to eat in front of people because she thought she might spill her food and everyone would laugh.

For Andrea, everyday activities became more and more difficult. Her problem wasn't getting any better, and she knew she needed to talk to an adult and get some help. She was relieved to find out that it *is* possible to overcome a phobia, if you get the help you need.

How do you know if you have social phobia? Here are some of the signs:

- You find it *really* hard to talk at school or in a group.

- You have very few friends because it isn't easy for you to be with other people.

- You're really scared of talking to your teacher or speaking up in class.

- You avoid most social situations, even the ones that sound fun.

- You're terrified of introducing yourself to people.

- You get very anxious when you're in a crowd.

- You avoid public bathrooms because you're scared someone might come in while you're there.

The tricky part is *lots* of people have these kinds of worries and fears—even adults. (In fact, the number one fear among most people is a fear of public speaking.) Ask yourself how strong or big your fear of social situations really is—does it feel like the fear is taking over your life? If so, you may have social phobia. Only an expert can tell you for sure, though.

# What to Do If You Have a Phobia

Remember, you need the help of an expert to know whether you're dealing with a phobia. If a doctor or therapist tells you that you have a phobia, what might happen next?

A lot depends on what kind of phobia you have. If you have a phobia about something you can avoid most of the time (like clowns or bears), you may not need to face your fear right now. Someday, you might even outgrow this phobia.

If your phobia is about something you can't avoid, however, you can work on finding ways to feel safe. Thirteen-year-old Chris had a phobia about storms, and it got so bad that he would spend hours watching the Weather Channel. He didn't want to go outside if he saw clouds in the sky.

Football star Ricky Williams, one of the best college football players ever, had social phobia. At age twenty-one, Ricky became the National Collegiate Athletic Association (NCAA) all-time leader in rushing yards and touchdowns. But when he played for the University of Dallas, he often felt anxious about being around people he didn't know, especially if they were looking at him. Whenever someone recognized him at a restaurant, his palms would start to sweat. He started missing football practices because he didn't want to be interviewed. His fear interfered with his love of the game. Finally, he went to a counselor to get some help. Since then, his love of football has returned and he has learned to handle his fears. He even went pro and played with the Miami Dolphins.

His family helped him cope with his phobia by getting him a weather warning radio and a home weather set—tools that helped Chris feel safer. Although he still worried about the weather, he started to gain more control over his fear. After a while, he was able to go outdoors again and have fun.

If you're dealing with social phobia, you probably need the help of a counselor, therapist, or doctor to learn ways to deal with it. It may take weeks or even months to overcome your phobia with expert help. If you have questions about what it's like to see a counselor or another expert, take a look at chapter 11.

Often, counselors and therapists use something called a Fear Scale, which is a way of working through a fear bit by bit. (You'll find a section on Fear Scales in chapter 4.) If you have a fear that bothers you a lot, the best cure is to face it a little at a time, until you beat it. This gets your body and mind used to the thing you're afraid of so that you don't react so strongly.

Another technique counselors and therapists use is called "flooding." Flooding is a way to face a fear head on, and it's one of the hardest techniques for fighting fears and phobias. *It's definitely not something to try on your own!* Here's how flooding works: If you have a bug phobia, you would let an ant or some other bug crawl on you—no matter how much it freaked you out. It would feel really scary at first, but the longer you were able to let the ant crawl on you, the less afraid you'd feel. It's called "flooding" because instead of avoiding what scares you, you're forcing yourself to let it wash over you, sort of like a flood. The expert guiding the technique would focus on helping you feel calm and safe. After repeating the technique again and again, your body would eventually stop going on Red Alert every time.

■ ■ ■

Fighting a phobia isn't easy, but it can be done. To help yourself stay stronger and calmer as you face your fear, try some of the Fear Chasers and Worry Erasers from chapter 3. See which ones help you the most, and then use them as often as needed.

## Chapter 6

# Fear of Being Away from Family Grown-ups

## (Separation Anxiety)

Many kids get scared when they're home alone, especially if they're at the age when they don't need baby-sitters anymore. Even those kids who still have a baby-sitter might get scared after their mom or dad leaves. But for some, having a parent leave the house—even for a short time—causes a huge amount of fear and anxiety. Intense worries about being separated from family grown-ups is called separation anxiety.

■ ■ ■

Eleven-year-old Tong got very nervous whenever his parents left him with a baby-sitter. He'd sit by the window for hours waiting for them to come home. As he waited, he thought of all sorts of bad things that could happen. He even had nightmares about his mom and dad going away. His stomach and head hurt just thinking about it, and sometimes he threw up from the stress. Whenever his parents said they were going somewhere, Tong would cry and beg them to stay with him.

Nine-year-old **Selena** had a similar problem with being away from her mom. When she had to go to school, she would throw a huge tantrum because she was scared to leave her mom. Sometimes, Selena screamed until her mom let her stay home.

■ ■ ■

If you sometimes feel worried about being home by yourself or being away from your dad or mom, that's normal. But if your fear is so intense that it lasts for weeks or longer, you may have separation anxiety. Some kids who have this problem find it very difficult to go to school or make friends. Often, they're too afraid to sleep in their own bed; they beg to sleep with their parents or on the floor next to them. Some kids find it hard to be left alone in any room in their home, even if a parent is in the next room.

Only a doctor or therapist can say for sure if you have separation anxiety. That's why it's so important to talk to an adult and get some expert help.

How do you know if you have separation anxiety? Here are some of the signs:

- You avoid overnight activities like slumber parties, camp, or just sleeping at a friend's home.

- You grab onto your mom or dad when it's time to say good-bye, and you find it hard to let go.

- You feel really scared that something bad will happen to you or to your parents if you're away from each other.

- You still worry, even if you know your dad or mom always comes back.

- You're afraid to go to school or to after-school activities. The fear is so strong that you avoid going by saying you're sick or throwing tantrums.

If you think you have separation anxiety, you may wonder how it started and why. Maybe it's because your mom or dad had anxiety problems when they were your age, which means you're more likely to as well. Or, perhaps you once got lost when you were younger and couldn't find your parents right away, and that triggered a fear of separation. Maybe your fears started because you moved to a new home and you were scared about making friends and starting at a new school. Separation anxiety can worsen if your family moves a lot.

If you're terribly afraid to go to school but you don't mind being away from your family at other times, you may have SCHOOL PHOBIA, which means you're scared of what happens to you at school. You can read more about phobias in chapter 5.

Maybe you've been moved from one home to another as part of being in foster care or getting adopted. If that's happened to you, you may find it hard to trust that the adults in your life will be there when you need them. You may worry that every time you leave home, you'll be taken to a new home.

Kids sometimes have separation anxiety after their parents separate or get a divorce. It's normal to cling to one or both parents at first. But if you still feel very anxious after a month or so, it may be a sign of separation anxiety.

Kids who have been physically hurt or sexually abused often feel more afraid to be away from their parents. If this has happened to you, you might not feel safe because you've been hurt before. If someone in your family has died, this can cause separation anxiety, too. You may fear that other people in your family will die and that you'll be left alone.

# What to Do If You Have Separation Anxiety

You probably know that having separation anxiety makes you miss out on fun things in life. The worries can cause stomachaches and headaches, which may cause you to miss days from school. The more days you miss, the harder it is to leave your parents again to return to school.

What you may not realize, though, is that your separation anxiety is hard not only for you but for the grown-ups who take care of you. Maybe your mom or dad has had to take time off from work to be with you when you're scared, or stay home with you instead of going somewhere in the evening. Or, maybe you fight with your family every morning before going to school. Sometimes, parents get upset with their kids when they have separation anxiety, and may even blame them for the problem. This makes the situation even harder to deal with.

Both you and your family will have an easier time if you learn to handle your separation anxiety. You can do this with the help of a counselor or another expert, or you can try some of the following ideas. You may also want to look at the Fear Chasers and Worry Erasers in chapter 3 for general tips on calming down.

1. **Make a plan.** Talk with your family grown-ups about a plan to help you feel safe while they're away. If they're going away for a few hours, ask them to take a cell phone, if they have one, so you can call them. Or, they can promise to call you every hour or two until they come home. Keeping a family photo close to you can help. Look at it when you need a reminder that everyone is safe, and know that you'll be

together again soon. Instead of worrying, focus on how much you'll enjoy seeing your dad and mom when they return.

2. **Make a list of good reasons not to worry.** Write down as many reasons as you can think of for not worrying, such as, "The grown-ups who take care of me always come back," or "I have fun with my sitter." Read the ideas aloud. Say them as if you really believe them to be true, even if that isn't how you feel—at least not yet. Thinking positive like this can help.

3. **Practice being separated from your parents one step at a time.** Start by asking them to leave for just five or ten minutes. While they're gone, use the ideas above to stay calm. You can do deep breathing or try other Fear Chasers and Worry Erasers from chapter 3. Once you feel comfortable with your dad and mom being gone for a short time, increase the amount little by little. Build up to twenty minutes, and then thirty. Keep going until you've lowered your anxiety level and are no longer as scared to see your mom and dad leave. (You may still worry a bit, even after days or weeks of practicing like this. It takes time. Your goal is for your anxiety to become low enough that you can manage it.)

4. **Plan fun things to do.** To keep your mind off of your worries, have lots of activities lined up while your parents are gone. You can watch a favorite movie or TV show (nothing scary, though), read, play video games, talk with

friends on the phone, have a friend over, or play board games with your baby-sitter. Work off some tension by exercising.

5.  **If you're afraid to go to school, write a plan.**
    You'll need to work together with your family
    adults, your teacher, and your principal. Create
    a plan—in writing—that tells you what steps to
    take when you get worried. They might include
    having the same person take you to school each
    day—preferably someone who won't let you
    put up a fight. Another step may be
    to visit the school counselor if you feel
    too afraid to stay in class. You might
    also take a break from class and call a
    family adult from the principal's office.
    Once everyone agrees to the plan, sign it
    together to make it official.

6.  **Create a reward chart.** Give yourself
    rewards when you make progress; this gives
    you a goal and something to look forward to.
    The rewards can be as simple as going some-
    place fun with your family or buying yourself a
    little gift. Just be sure not to "punish" yourself
    when you don't handle your anxiety well.

## Noah's Story

When Noah was nine, he worried whenever his
parents went out to dinner together. Even though
they were gone only a few hours and his older
brother was baby-sitting, Noah still worried. He sat
by the window looking for his parents and watched

the news to see if they had been in a car accident. He paced back and forth in the living room, waiting for them to come home. Noah and his family decided to make a plan to help him handle his fears. Here's what they did:

- His parents had a cell phone, and they would always call him when they reached the place they were going. Noah was allowed to call once every hour to check on them.

- Noah and his brother agreed to play Noah's favorite video games together while their parents were away. They also rented funny movies and shot some hoops outside while waiting for their parents to return. The exercise helped Noah calm down.

- Noah kept a picture of his parents on the table. Each time he saw their picture, Noah would repeat to himself, "I know they're fine. I don't need to worry."

■ ■ ■

With separation anxiety, it's important to have a plan that the whole family can use. Keep in mind that you'll need to keep practicing for the plan to work—results don't happen overnight!

# Chapter 7

# Constant Worrying for Months at a Time

## (Generalized Anxiety Disorder)

Eleven-year-old **Calvin** worries a lot about how he'll do at school. He also worries about making friends, doing his chores correctly, and getting hurt on his bike. There's always *something* he's worried about. Even though he knows there's no need to worry so much about these things, he can't stop himself. He wishes he could stop being so anxious all the time.

■ ■ ■

**Carla,** age ten, constantly worries about "what ifs" like "What if I don't make a goal in soccer, what if my teammates hate me, and what if my mom and dad can't pay the bills?" She's a big worrier, and all those doubts in her mind make it hard for her to get through the day. Even when she's playing soccer, a sport she loves, Carla can't get the worries out of her mind.

Most kids are able to handle the worries of every-day life without getting too upset. They can put their worries aside while they're doing homework or having fun outside. But people with Generalized Anxiety Disorder (or GAD, for short) have worries that are very deep and hard to ignore. Sometimes, just the idea of going through the day can be worrisome for someone who has this problem.

If you're a worrier, you may have lots of anxious thoughts about the future. You may feel scared about growing up and all the responsibilities you'll have as an adult. On the other hand, you may worry a lot but not about specific things—you just feel worried and you don't know why. Constant worrying can make it hard to concentrate or to relax after a busy day at school. The results of all this worrying? You might start getting poor grades, or find it difficult to make friends, or have a lot of arguments with your dad or mom.

If your worrying has been going on for more than six months, you may have Generalized Anxiety Disorder. People who have GAD *can* get control of their worries— if they get the help they need.

Where does GAD come from? Some people seem to be born worriers. Just as some people are taller than others, some are more

Only a doctor or therapist can say for sure if you have GAD. That's why it's so important to talk to an adult and get some expert help.

anxious, even from the time when they're very young. If your parents or other family members have Generalized Anxiety Disorder, you're more likely to have the same problem yourself.

Another cause of GAD is having an experience that scares you deeply. If you have ever been badly hurt or been a victim of violence, for example, you may end up with GAD. Or, maybe you have a habit of thinking that bad things are going to occur more often than they do, which also can lead to GAD.

According to scientists who study GAD, the most common things kids who have it worry about are:
- their health
- how they do in school
- being physically hurt
- disasters, such as tornadoes, floods, or terrorist attacks

How do you know if you have GAD? Here are the main signs:

■ You feel fidgety or restless. Maybe your legs or your hands are shaky, or you're always moving some part of your body (even when you're supposed to be sitting still).

■ You get tired easily, even when you've had enough sleep. Your lack of energy makes it hard to do things you want or need to do.

■ You have trouble concentrating, or your mind seems to go blank. You may forget things that you normally wouldn't forget.

■ You're irritable or cranky—it seems that every little thing bothers you.

■ Your muscles are tense, tight, or hurting. You can't seem to relax.

■ You have trouble falling asleep at night or staying asleep.

Here are some other signs of GAD:

■ stomachaches

■ having to pee more often than usual

■ diarrhea

■ feeling lightheaded or dizzy, or turning red in the face

■ cold and clammy hands

■ a dry mouth

■ sweating a lot

■ being *hypervigilant,* which means you're always on the lookout for signs of danger, even when danger is unlikely

If you have some of the symptoms described above, you may have GAD. On the other hand, many of the symptoms here could be signs of other problems, such as depression. It's best to talk to a doctor or an expert first, so you can get the help you need.

# What to Do If You Have GAD

Often, kids who have GAD feel sad—because it's hard to enjoy life when so many worries are spinning through their mind. Kids who are too anxious to join in with other kids may end up not only sad but lonely, too. If you feel sad and lonely, talk to an adult you trust. Opening up about your feelings can really help a lot.

Having GAD may also leave you feeling upset or angry, especially if you're wondering why other kids aren't bothered by their worries like you are. You may feel helpless or lose hope that your worries will ever go away. But here's the good news: There's a lot you can do to overcome your worries!

One good way to help yourself is to work on the things in your life that you *can* control. For example, if GAD is affecting your performance on a team, talk to your coach about what's going on. Tell your coach

that you want to stay in the game but could use some extra help with keeping your focus. Don't stop going to practice, even when you're feeling stressed. Remember that exercise helps you work off excess energy and helps clear your mind. If GAD is making it hard for you to concentrate at school, get some extra help with your homework or begin working with a tutor. This will help you keep your grades up and give you the feeling that you're doing something positive.

You can also take a look at the Fear Chasers and Worry Erasers in chapter 3. There you'll find ten ways to outsmart your worries and take good care of yourself. Because GAD involves worrying a lot of the time about many different things, you'll need to work on taming those worries every day.

You may find it helpful to work with a counselor or another expert who can show you other techniques for handling your anxiety. If you have questions about what it's like to visit a counselor or therapist, see chapter 11. Sometimes, kids who have GAD take medicine that relieves their anxiety. Only a doctor or another expert can tell you if medicine will help in your situation, though.

■ ■ ■

The best thing you can do if you have GAD is to take action. Using the ideas you've read about here, you and your grown-up helper can come up with a game plan—and get started as soon as today.

# Chapter 8

# Fear That Stops You in Your Tracks

## (Panic Attacks)

Maybe you've had something like this happen: You're at school or outside and, all of a sudden, your heart starts pounding and you have trouble catching your breath. You start shaking, and you're afraid that you're either going crazy or having a heart attack and about to die. You don't know what's happening to you, so it's even scarier. After a few minutes, your body returns to normal but you're still upset and confused afterward.

What happened? It's called a panic attack, and it can happen to people of all ages—both kids and adults.

When you have a panic attack, the anxiety is so strong that it seems to take over your whole body. You may feel short of breath or have trouble understanding everything you're feeling at that moment. Even if the feelings don't last long, they can be terrifying.

Panic attacks are more likely to happen during stressful times, such as when you're going to a new school or have to perform in front of others. But sometimes, one of these attacks just happens; one minute you're feeling fine, and the next you're in a total panic. Most panic attacks don't last too long—usually ten minutes or less.

How do you know if you're having a panic attack? Here are the main signs:

- You feel your heart pounding hard, and your chest hurts.

- You may get sweaty all over.

- You begin to tremble or shake.

- You have trouble catching your breath (also called *hyperventilating*).

- You feel like you're choking on something.

- Your stomach hurts.

- You get dizzy or lightheaded; you feel like you're about to faint.

- You feel as if everything around you is unreal, or like you're watching yourself.

- You're scared that you're losing control or going crazy.

- You feel tingly or numb in your fingers or toes.

- You start feeling too cold (the chills) or too hot (hot flashes).

- You feel as if you're about to die.

There's also something called *panic disorder,* which means you have panic attacks over and over. Some people have panic attacks every week; others have them every day for a week, and then have no attacks for months. Sometimes, people have "mini-attacks," where they panic but have only a few of the symptoms. With panic disorder, the fear of another attack is often the worst part. You may start avoiding people and places, because you're scared that you'll panic again.

If you've had what you think is a panic attack, be sure to get a check-up with your doctor. He or she can make sure your symptoms aren't related to an illness.

# Five Causes of Panic Attacks

There's no doubt about it: panic attacks are frightening. They won't hurt you, but knowing that doesn't always make them less scary. So, what causes panic attacks? A few things, such as:

Only a doctor or therapist can say for sure if you have panic disorder. That's why it's so important to talk to an adult and get some expert help.

**1. Family history.** Panic attacks run in families. If you have panic attacks, chances are another one of your family members has the same problem.

2.  **Problems with a brain chemical.** People with panic disorder may have less of the important brain chemical called *serotonin*. Medicines that help serotonin work harder often help lessen anxiety and panic. (These medicines have to be prescribed by a doctor or another expert first.)

3.  **Fearful situations.** Being scared about going to a new school or moving to a new neighborhood can cause a panic attack. Also, worrying about having a panic attack can sometimes bring one on.

4.  **Feeling stressed out.** When you're worried that you can't handle things in your life, your stress level goes up. This extra stress can lead to a panic attack.

5.  **Adrenaline reaction.** Any of the above causes may bring on an increase in adrenaline, which is a hormone your body uses to give you energy. The adrenaline makes your heart beat faster and speeds up your breathing. During a panic attack, your body reacts as if you're in danger (even if you aren't).

Since you never know when panic will strike, you may fear going out in public where people can see you having an attack. You may be afraid to go to school or other places you have to go. Combined with this fear, you may also feel sad and guilty— especially if you blame yourself for having panic attacks. But the panic attacks aren't your fault; they can happen to anyone. Just because you have panic attacks doesn't mean you're "weak."

Some people who have panic attacks may fear leaving their home at all. They only feel calm at home, and so they avoid going out in public. A fear like this is called *agoraphobia*. You can read more about phobias in chapter 5.

# What to Do If You Have a Panic Attack

The next time you feel a panic attack coming, tell yourself you're strong enough to handle it. Once you've learned some ways to deal with panic attacks, you'll be able to get through them more easily. You may find it helpful to work with a counselor or another expert who can guide you. For more about that, see chapter 11.

1.  **Talk yourself through it.** Remind yourself that panic attacks aren't dangerous and only last a

short time. Instead of trying to fight it, tell yourself, "Okay, here it is again. I know it's just a panic attack. I'll let it happen and wait for it to be over." Trying to fight a panic attack can make it worse. By letting it happen, the attack will end sooner. Here are some more words for talking yourself through it:

■ "I don't like these feelings, but I can handle them."

■ "I can ride this out."

■ "I've handled it before, and I can do it again."

■ "This isn't dangerous, and I can deal with it."

■ "I'm just having a panic attack—it will pass."

Even if you feel short of breath, remind yourself that you won't stop breathing— because your brain won't let that happen. If your lungs feel tight and you're not getting enough air, your brain will force you to breathe. (If you don't believe this, do an experiment. Hold your breath for a minute. At some point, you'll feel a strong urge to get more air and you won't be able to hold it any longer. The same thing happens during a panic attack.)

Know that you won't go crazy or totally lose control because of a panic attack. If you're panicking, the most likely thing that will happen is you'll try to escape the situation by running away. You won't lose complete control, even if it *feels* like you will.

2.  **Stop it before it gets worse.** Pay attention to the early signs of a panic attack. You may notice your heart beating faster, nervous feelings, and your muscles getting tight. If you feel an attack coming on, take a break from what you're doing. For example, go outside and get some fresh air so you won't feel trapped. Walk around or get some exercise to work off the adrenaline that's building up. If you're short of breath, breathe more deeply, filling the bottom part of your lungs first and then the top part. Breathe slowly and gently to calm down. Chapter 3 explains deep breathing in more detail.

    You can also start talking to someone, which may take your mind off your anxiety. Another way to get your mind off the panic is to do something simple, such as chewing gum or grabbing a snack. You might also try counting things, like the number of chairs in your classroom or the number of kids—anything you can think of to distract yourself.

3.  **Wait until it passes.** Remember that the best cure for a panic attack is time. After panicking for a while, your body will start to calm down on its own. Your breathing will slow, your heart won't beat so fast, and your muscles will start to relax. You may be uncomfortable for a few minutes or longer, but then it will be over.

Once you understand panic attacks, you probably won't be as upset when the next one occurs. Just let it happen and be patient while your body gets around to turning on its own calming response.

■ ■ ■

You can reduce panic attacks by keeping your stress under control and using the Fear Chasers and Worry Erasers from chapter 3. In particular, try deep breathing and muscle relaxation so you're calmer each day.

# Chapter 9

# Thoughts and Actions You Just Can't Stop

## (Obsessive-Compulsive Disorder)

Maybe you've heard of something called Obsessive-Compulsive Disorder, or OCD for short. Just as its name suggests, this disorder causes someone to have obsessions or compulsions—which means odd thoughts, feelings, and behaviors. Although everyone may have strange thoughts or do unusual things some of the time, someone with OCD can't stop.

Obsessions are thoughts that won't go away, no matter how hard you try. They're usually worries—*really* intense worries about germs or about something bad happening. Compulsions are actions that you feel you *must* do. You may know they don't make sense and you may not really want to do them, but you feel that you have no choice. It seems as if doing these behaviors is the only way to stop the thoughts.

■ ■ ■

For example, eleven-year-old **Michael** does odd things over and over, even though he knows they're weird. When he closes the refrigerator door, he feels that he has do it five times. If he doesn't close it five times, he worries that the food will spoil and he'll get sick. He also lines up his baseball cards in perfect order on his desk and gets very upset if anyone messes them up. Michael rechecks his cards many times every day. Before leaving his house, he counts to ten, and at each even number (two, four, etc.), he touches the doorknob. He thinks something bad might happen if he doesn't.

■ ■ ■

Thirteen-year-old **Jonathan** also has OCD, and he has to do things a certain way to keep from getting anxious. If he chews his food five times on the left side of his mouth, he has to do it five times on the right side. If he messes up his counting, he has to start all over again. Jonathan knows this doesn't make sense; it takes him longer to eat than most kids, but he can't stop himself. If he tries to fight the compulsions, he gets even more anxious.

■ ■ ■

**Lanie,** age nine, is obsessed with germs. She can't eat any food that has been touched by someone else, because of the germs. She can't use a public bathroom because she's scared the germs there will harm her, so she'll only go to the bathroom at home. This is a serious problem when she's at school or outside all day. She worries the whole time that she'll wet her pants in front of people.

*Everyone* has worries. And lots of people have super-stitions (beliefs about preventing bad luck or getting good luck). But for people with OCD, the worries and beliefs—and the behav-iors that go with them—are really extreme.

Maybe you sometimes count to calm yourself down. Or, maybe you sometimes do little things to bring yourself good luck—like carry-ing a charm in your pocket or throwing salt over your shoulder. Just because you do these things doesn't mean you have OCD. Remember, OCD is a serious problem, causing thoughts and behaviors that you can't stop no matter how hard you try. If the thoughts and actions take up a lot of your time, worry you a lot, or keep you from getting other things done, they are a sign that you need to tell someone what's going on.

Only a doctor or therapist can say for sure if you have OCD. That's why it's so important to talk to an adult and get some expert help.

How do you know if you have OCD? Here are some of the signs of obsessive thoughts:

- You worry constantly about a certain thing—like germs, catching a disease, or someone breaking into your home.

■ You hear a certain song over and over in your head. (This happens to everyone at times, but if you can't get the song out of your mind no matter what you do, it could be a sign of a problem.)

■ You have frequent thoughts about hurting or killing yourself or someone else. If you do, please talk to a family grown-up right away. Find someone you trust to talk to, so you can get the help you need.

■ You have constant doubts that you shut the door or zipped your backpack, or other such things. So you check and recheck, just to make sure.

■ You need to have things lined up just right, whether it's food or items on your desk or dresser.

■ You doubt your every move; for example, you think you're not walking through a doorway or closing the cabinets the "right way." You constantly think you didn't do it "right" or didn't do it at all.

■ You imagine bad things happening to you or your family. (These thoughts happen to everyone, so you have to ask yourself how often you have such ideas in your mind. If you have them almost all the time and can't stop them, they may be obsessive.)

Here are some signs of compulsive behaviors:

- You ask grown-ups or friends for something over and over again, and you don't give up if the answer is no. You just can't seem to stop asking, even if you know the answer will still be the same.

- You wash your hands ten times instead of once. You wash them until they are red and chapped, even though this hurts.

- You count things, such as cracks in a sidewalk or patterns on the ceiling, over and over.

- You check things again and again to make sure they are "right." For example, you check your homework over and over for mistakes, even though you didn't find any the first time.

- You touch things a certain number of times.

- You collect useless things, such as scraps of paper and candy wrappers.

- You can't throw anything away for fear of needing it again.

- You start all over again when you mess up, because you think that what you're doing has to be "perfect."

It can be scary if you have thoughts and behaviors like these and can't get rid of them. You might be scared to tell anyone about them, because you think you'll seem "crazy." But the best thing you can do to help yourself is talk to an adult about the problems you're having. There is help out there for people who have OCD.

## Jackie's Story

Jackie spends an hour in the bathroom every morning. She takes long showers because she has to wash herself four times. She also has to wash herself in a certain order: first her hair, then her arms, then her legs, then her feet. If she makes a mistake in the order, she has to start all over again.

Because of these behaviors, she is often late for school. Her parents get angry and frustrated that Jackie takes so long to get ready and often misses her bus. Her brothers and sisters complain that she spends too much time in the bathroom.

Jackie is too embarrassed to tell her parents about what's happening. She doesn't want to tell them about her need to do things a certain way, and how she can't stop herself from doing what she does. For a long time now, Jackie has been hiding her problem and trying to make excuses for her behavior. She really wants to tell her parents the truth, but she's afraid to. She thinks no one else in the world has such strange thoughts and behaviors, and that she must be the only one.

Obsessive thoughts and behaviors make it terribly difficult to get through the day. At times, you probably feel very frustrated and frightened by what's happening to you. You may be avoiding certain places and situations, because they make you more anxious. This can make it harder for you to do any of the things you like to do.

If you do have OCD, getting professional help is so important. Even if it's scary to ask for help, please talk to a family grown-up as soon as possible.

# What to Do
# If You Have OCD

Remember, you need the help of an expert to know whether you're dealing with OCD. If a doctor or therapist tells you that you have this problem, what might happen next?

It's possible that the expert you see will suggest that you take a medication to help balance the chemicals in your brain. People with OCD don't seem to have enough of a brain chemical called *serotonin*. If you get a prescription for a medication, you'll need to make sure that you take it just as the directions say to.

You might also work with a counselor or therapist who can help you with your worries and behaviors. (See chapter 11 for more about what it's like to go to counseling.) The expert you work with will have ideas for helping you. One of these ideas may be making a Fear Scale, an activity you can learn more about in chapter 4. The goal is to face your worries a little bit at a time, until you have more control over them.

A well-known therapist named John Marsh came up with many great ideas for helping people who have OCD. One simple idea of his is giving your problem a name. If you name it, you start thinking about it differently; you see it as something separate from you. In other words, *you* aren't the problem, the OCD is the problem—and you can take charge of it. Some kids name their OCD "Silly Worries" or "Terrible Troubles," but you can call it whatever you like.

Another idea that you and your counselor may try is something called "making a map" of your OCD. (John Marsh came up with this idea, too.) The goal is to list your obsessions and compulsions, and write down what makes each one better or worse. This gives you a picture of how much control your OCD has over you and your life. Once you have that picture, you and your counselor can try ideas for coping with each thought or behavior that gives you trouble.

Other ideas include "twisting" your compulsions or doing them in slow motion. So, instead of checking the door five times, you make a point of doing it four or six times. If you have to do things in a certain order, switch the order. Or, try doing the behaviors in slow motion so you have to think about your every move. Doing things differently takes some of the power out of your compulsions and puts you more in control.

It may also help you to choose a certain time of day that you call your Worry Time. So, instead of obsessing all day, you pick a time each day to worry and you give yourself fifteen minutes to a half hour to do nothing but worry. Try to put off any worrying until your time arrives. Once the time comes, sit down and let yourself worry about as many things as you want. You can write down all the thoughts and obsessions you have, if you'd like. Repeat this activity at the same time each day; this will help you give your mind a rest at other times.

Some kids find it helpful to keep a diary or journal of their OCD behavior. Each day, you can write about how you're coming along in your goal to control your OCD. Write down your thoughts and behaviors and how you're learning to cope with them. Share what you write with someone you trust. If you like the idea of keeping an OCD journal, here are some more ideas to try:

What ideas are you using to help get control of your OCD? How are these ideas working for you? Which ones work the best, and why?

What is your plan for tomorrow? What ideas do you plan to try if your thoughts and behaviors start up again?

Who do you talk to about your OCD? How does it feel to talk about it?

Write about your good days and bad days. (It's normal to have them.) What might you do to make the hard days easier on you?

■ ■ ■

The obsessions and compulsions that are part of OCD take up a lot of time and energy. They also leave you feeling different from everyone else. This is why it's so important to talk to a grown-up and get some help. It may take some time to find treatments that work for you, but it will be worth the effort. Don't give up!

# Chapter 10

# Stress and Fear from a Terrible Memory

## (Post-Traumatic Stress Disorder)

When something scary happens to you, it's normal to get really upset and frightened. If you have a bad fall on your skateboard, for example, you may remember how scared or hurt you felt, and it may be hard to get back on your skateboard again. But eventually, you do get back on and, at some point, you forget that you once fell.

But when very bad things happen—the kinds of things that don't happen to most kids—the feelings afterward can be deeply troubling. Anyone who has been in a bad accident or has been a victim of violence, for example, may have strong feelings that don't go away later. This can lead to what's known as Post-Traumatic Stress Disorder or PTSD.

The word *trauma* describes an event that leaves you feeling terrified or helpless. Witnessing a crime or being a victim of one is a good example. Having someone in your family get hurt or die is another example. Kids who have been through situations where they think they're going to die have experienced trauma. This can happen if you've been in a fire or some other disaster, if you've had someone in your family die, or if you've had a serious illness and were put in the hospital. Other types of trauma include abuse or being taken from your home and put into foster care.

ALERT!

Such events cause so much stress that your body and brain go on Red Alert (see chapter 2). Your first reaction during a trauma may be to feel really scared and helpless. You may try to hide or run away, or you may feel that you should do something—anything—to stop what's happening. Or, maybe you freeze and you can't move, even though you want to get yourself out of the traumatic situation.

All of these feelings may stay with you long after the trauma is over. If the trauma is *very* scary, your body may become numb (having no feelings at all) to protect you from your fear. This means you may not be able to enjoy anything the way you used to, even playing or laughing

The first time scientists learned about PTSD was from talking with soldiers who came back from the Vietnam War in the 1960s. These soldiers had a hard time adjusting to normal life after the terrible things they experienced in the war. The soldiers felt wound up and had horrible nightmares about things that happened to them in Vietnam. Later on, researchers figured out that people who experienced traumas like accidents or violence had many of the same problems as the soldiers. Experts still haven't figured out why some victims of trauma develop PTSD and others don't.

with friends. If you've had feelings of intense fear or if you've felt numb for more than a month after the trauma ended, you may have Post-Traumatic Stress Disorder.

How do you know if you have PTSD? In the weeks after a trauma, there are three major signs, and each one can show up in several different ways:

1. **You relive the event:**

■ You keep thinking about what happened. You get upset when you think about it or are reminded of it. You picture scary things in your head, and it's hard to stop these images.

■ You have bad dreams about the event. The dreams happen over and over and don't stop.

■ You have flashbacks where you start acting or feeling as if the trauma is happening all over again. Sometimes, this happens just after you wake up.

■ Your heart starts racing and you breathe faster, because your body feels afraid all over again. This can happen any time that you're reminded of the trauma. If you were in a car accident, just seeing a car may leave you scared and upset.

2. **You feel numb or avoid anything that reminds you of what happened:**

■ You try to avoid thinking or talking about the trauma because it upsets you too much. You ignore any feelings about it or even try to pretend it never happened.

■ You avoid doing things, going places, or being around people that remind you of the trauma.

■ You may forget part of what happened; this is your brain's way of trying to protect you. By not remembering, you don't have to think about it.

■ You don't want to do fun things as much as you did before. Maybe you don't enjoy them, or it seems easier to lie around and do nothing.

■ You feel that you don't fit in with others anymore and you feel alone when others are around. You might feel different from everyone else because of what happened to you.

■ You don't feel much of anything—not happy, sad, or worried. Being numb is your body's way of protecting you by shutting off most of your feelings.

■ You think you won't live long and that you may die earlier than everyone else.

### 3. Your body can't relax—you're always wound up:

■ You have trouble falling or staying asleep. Maybe you can't turn off your thoughts at night. Or, you may be afraid to fall asleep because you think you won't be able to protect yourself if something bad happens.

■ You're irritable and you get angry easily. Little things upset you.

■ You have trouble concentrating. Your mind is always thinking about other things, which makes it hard to pay attention in school or do homework.

■ You're always looking around and expecting something bad to happen. You're on alert all the time, which can wear you out.

■ You're very jumpy if anyone sneaks up on you, even accidentally. This makes it hard to relax or fall asleep.

Only a doctor or therapist can say for sure if you have PTSD. That's why it's so important to talk to an adult and get some expert help.

# What to Do If You Have PTSD

Eleven-year-old Alicia was beaten up by two bullies at school before her teachers stopped them. Now she has trouble sleeping, gets angry a lot, and has a hard time paying attention to her schoolwork. Every morning before school, Alicia gets stomachaches and asks her parents to let her stay home. At school, her mind sometimes goes blank. When she walks in the hallways, she looks everywhere to make sure the bullies aren't waiting for her. She knows the girls who did this to her got in trouble and can't hurt her anymore, but it's almost like she's reliving the experience of being beaten up. She just doesn't know what to do.

Maybe you've had an experience like Alicia's. Something really scary happened to you, and even though it's been a while, you can't seem to get past it. What should you do?

What to do depends, in part, on whether anyone knows about the trauma you've experienced. If something happened to you and you haven't told anyone else, it's time to talk to an adult you trust. Talking about your painful experience is the first step toward healing. You can talk to your dad or mom, your teacher or school counselor, a religious leader, or someone else you trust.

If people already know about what happened, you may believe that there's no point in talking about it further. But talking can help. It may be hard to put what you're feeling into words, and you may feel scared that talking will bring up the difficult feelings again. The more you talk about it, the less upset you'll feel. Don't keep your feelings bottled up inside, where they may get worse.

You might have to talk about what happened every day or every week before you start feeling better. Talk about it as often as you need to, because it gives your body and mind a chance to heal.

It may also help to draw or write about the trauma. You can draw/write about what actually happened or how you wish it could have happened differently. Both can help you feel better about it. Share your words and pictures with a grown-up who can help you work through your feelings.

There are other techniques for dealing with trauma,

including making a Fear Scale (see chapter 4), which can help you face your fears little by little. It's best to work on a Fear Scale with adult help, though. Find a grown-up you trust and give the Fear Scale a try, if you feel like you may be ready for that. You may even decide it's a good idea to see a counselor or another expert who can help you learn to handle what you've been through. For more about counseling, see chapter 11.

■ ■ ■

Just as physical wounds take time to heal, emotional wounds take time, too. No one can promise you that you'll never have another trauma. But by talking about what happened and practicing other ways to help yourself, you will feel better and stronger—and ready to move on.

## Chapter 11

# How Experts Can Help

Practicing the ideas in this book can help you a lot, but it's possible that you'll need other help, too. If you're still struggling with your fears and worries after trying the ideas or if you have a problem that is too big to handle without expert help, you may need to go to counseling or therapy. A counselor or therapist is a person you can talk to about your worries and fears. Below are some of the most frequently asked questions about counseling, as well as answers that may help.

## #1: What happens in counseling?

The counselor will listen to your problems and give you ideas about how to handle them. Counseling sessions usually last for almost an hour. Your counselor will ask you questions to learn about your worries. Together, you can come up with ideas that will help you, and then you can practice the ideas at home. The counselor is also there to answer any questions you have about your worries or other problems in your life.

It may take time for counseling to work. A lot depends on how well you get along with your counselor and whether you try the ideas he or she suggests. Give this person a chance, but if the sessions don't seem to be working for you, talk to your dad or mom. You may need to find a different counselor until you meet with one that you really like.

## #2: Who will be there?

You can go to the sessions alone, or you can bring along a family adult if you want to. Having a family grown-up there may help you feel more comfortable, and that person can learn ways to help you at home. Sometimes, older brothers or sisters might be included in a session, if you'd like that to happen.

## #3: Why do I have to talk about my problems?

No one will make you talk if you don't want to. Some kids feel embarrassed about telling their problems to a stranger. Others don't want to admit to having problems. This is normal. It may take a while to get to know your counselor, and you may not say much at first. After you feel comfortable, it will be easier to talk. Remember that talking about your problems is much more helpful than keeping them bottled up inside.

The counselor can't help you if you keep your problems a secret. If you're scared or angry about meeting with the counselor, start out by telling the counselor your feelings. If your counselor gives you an idea that you don't like, tell the counselor how you feel about it and ask for a different idea. This way, your counselor can think of different strategies that you might like better.

## #4: Won't everyone find out about my problem?

Your visits with your counselor are confidential, which means that your counselor isn't allowed to tell anyone else about your problems. The only time a counselor has to tell your parents about what you say is if you tell the counselor that you're thinking about hurting yourself or someone else, or if someone is hurting you. This is to make sure no one gets hurt, including you.

You can decide if you want to tell other people in your family what you're learning in counseling. And it's up to you whether or not you tell your friends about what's going on. If you have friends you trust, it may help you to talk to them about your fears and worries. Maybe your friends can help you.

## #5: Does my mom or dad have to talk to the counselor, too?

If your parents brought you to a counselor, this probably means they're not sure how to help you with your worries and fears. Your counselor can explain the problem to your parents so they can understand you better and give you the help you need. The counselor can also talk to them about better ways to help you, if what they're doing isn't helping or is making things worse for you. Counseling often works best if parents are involved, too. If you want your counselor to keep some of the things you say confidential, be sure to let him or her know that.

## #6: Does my teacher have to know about this?

If your worries or fears aren't affecting your schoolwork, no one at school needs to know that you're in counseling. If your fears involve school, your counselor may want to talk with your teacher to give suggestions on how to help you. By law, your parents have to give the counselor permission to talk with anyone at your school. If you don't want this to happen, let your counselor and your parents know.

## #7: How long do I have to go to the counselor?

Some kids may need to go just a few times, but others may need to go every week for a few months or longer. It depends on what the problem is, how hard you work at it, and how quickly you improve. Be patient, because it can take a while for counseling to help. Sometimes, counseling isn't enough and you may need medication as well. If you think counseling isn't helping, for whatever reason, talk to your parents and your counselor about it.

## #8: What about medication?

If you get so anxious that you can't get rid of your worries no matter how hard you try or if you have one of the problems described in Part 2 of this book, you may need medication to help you. Medications for these problems are designed to help the brain chemicals that affect how you feel and act. Only a doctor or psychiatrist can tell you whether you might need to take a medication. The doctor will ask you questions about your worries and figure out which medication will work best in your situation.

Some medications can cause side effects, such as headaches, stomachaches, or sleepiness. They can make your mouth dry, make you yawn a lot, or cause you to gain weight. Sometimes, a medication may actually make your problems worse. Because people react in different ways to different medications, there's no way to tell how a medication may affect you. If you have side effects you don't like, talk to your parents and counselor. The side effects may go away after a few weeks as your body gets used to the medication.

It's important to take the medication the way your doctor tells you, which usually means every day. Don't stop taking it on your own or take more of it, as this can cause problems. If you have questions about the medication or want to take more or less, *always* talk to your parents and your doctor first.

## #9: What if we can't afford counseling?

It is possible to find free or low-cost counseling services, depending on your family's needs. You may want to start by talking to your school counselor or your principal about special services that may be available through your school district. Your dad or mom can look in the Yellow Pages for low-cost counseling services, or contact a county social worker for more information. Depending on what type of medical insurance your family has, it's possible that the insurance company will help pay the cost of some counseling sessions.

## #10: What more can I do?

At the end of this book, you'll find a "Note to Grown-ups" that you can share with your parent or another family adult who can help you manage your worries and fears. On pages 118–119, you'll find a list of other resources that may be of help to you and your family, too.

# Resources

*Don't Pop Your Cork on Mondays!* by Adolph Moser (Kansas City, MO: Landmark Editions, Inc., 1988). Learn the causes of stress and how it affects you. Keeping your stress under control can also help you control your worries.

*Magic Island: Relaxation for Kids* by B. Mehling, M. Highstein, & R. Delamarter (Calabasas, CA: California Publications (BMI), 1990). With calming background music, this audiocassette tells of a hot air balloon journey to a magic island. Guided imagery and deep breathing instructions help you to relax, forget about your worries, and even fall asleep.

*Up and Down the Worry Hill: A Children's Book About Obsessive-Compulsive Disorder and Its Treatment* by Aureen Pinto Wagner (Rochester, NY: Lighthouse Press, 2000). This short, easy-to-read book gives you (and friends and family) an idea of what OCD is like from a kid's point of view. Also has an adult companion book: *What to Do When Your Child Has Obsessive-Compulsive Disorder: Strategies and Solutions.*

**KidsHealth**
*www.kidshealth.org/kid*
This site for kids can help you learn more about fears and worries, and other stuff about staying healthy, dealing with feelings, and handling medical problems.

# A NOTE TO GROWN-UPS

It can be tough to see your child struggle with anxiety and the problems it causes. Taking the extra time to deal again and again with a child's worries can be exhausting. You may feel frustrated when, despite your reassurance, your child continues to be fearful. Yet your child needs your continued support. This chapter will offer you some practical information and ideas so you can help more effectively.

## How Children React When They're Fearful

Different children respond to their fears in different ways. Some kids are very open about them, others show their anxieties and fears in their behavior. For example:

- denying that there's a problem (this occurs especially with boys)
- becoming or seeming emotionally numb
- playing more aggressively
- frequently re-creating traumatic situations during play
- avoiding new situations
- developing bodily symptoms such as aches, pains, or appetite and sleep disturbances

## How to Help Your Child

**Give lots of encouragement.** Give your child as much encouragement as possible for her attempts to practice the exercises in this book. If she has trouble or feels like giving up, reassure her that with time and practice, you're confident she will eventually learn to overcome her fears.

**Set an example for handling situations without anxiety.** Anxious children are often overly sensitive to their parents' feelings. If you're afraid of social situations and respond by avoiding them or panicking, your child notices. If you overreact to your child's cuts and bruises, your child senses and takes on your anxiety. Dealing with your own worries and fears will help your child greatly.

Most of the information in this book also applies to adults with anxiety problems; you can also seek counseling if you think it might help you.

**Make exercise a family activity.** Exercise can be very helpful for anxious children, but many of them don't want to do it alone. Ask your child to join you in doing something active, such as a walk, a bike ride, or chores.

**Let your child know it's okay to express feelings.** Many children don't like talking about how they feel. Reassure your child that though it may be hard to talk about strong emotions, the more he does so, the sooner he will start feeling better. Children are sensitive to how adults react when they do share their feelings, so it's important to show that you are accepting of those feelings. If you react with alarm or by criticizing, making fun, ignoring, or yelling, your child may stop confiding in you.

**Be a coach.** It's more helpful to act as a coach to your child than it is to just tell her what to do. Help your child think of ways to overcome her fear or anxiety.

**Consider reward systems.** For some children, rewards can be an extra incentive to do the hard work necessary to overcome fears. For other children, a reward system can seem like another opportunity to fail. Ask your child first if he would like to try a reward system—don't push it. Reassure him that if it doesn't work, it doesn't mean he has failed. It just means you need to try something different.

Reward systems work best for younger children, up to about age 12. Make a day-by-day chart of the behaviors you want to encourage. Decide on how many points, from 1 to 5, your child can earn with each behavior. Make a separate list of rewards your child would like to earn and the number of points needed to earn each one. Then, at the end of every day, review the chart together. At the end of the week, your child can "spend" the points she has earned. Some children may need to get their rewards more often, even daily, in order for a chart to work. See what works best.

For example:

| BEHAVIOR GOAL | SAT | SUN | MON | TUES | WED | THR | FRI |
|---|---|---|---|---|---|---|---|
| Stayed at school all day | | | | | | | |
| Did deep breathing | | | | | | | |
| Was able to stop worrying | | | | | | | |
| Asked for help | | | | | | | |

## When Is Counseling Needed?

If you and your child try the ideas in this book and nothing seems to work, it's wise to seek professional help. If your child is having many physical symptoms, such as aches and pains, first take him to the pediatrician for a checkup. Sometimes there are medical reasons for physical symptoms, and this possibility should be ruled out.

## Who Offers Counseling?

Mental health professionals such as psychologists, social workers, and licensed professional counselors can provide therapy for your child, if needed. They can diagnose the problem and decide whether your child's worries are normal or whether the problem is more serious. Be sure to ask what kind of training and experience the therapist has in working with children with anxiety disorders. If you aren't sure where to start looking for a therapist, ask the school guidance counselor or a health-care professional for recommendations. You can also check the phone book under Mental Health Services or Counselors or Psychologists. The list of organizations on page 119 may also be of assistance. Let the agency know if cost is a concern; ask if free or low-cost services are available.

## How Does Counseling Work?

*Cognitive behavioral therapy* is an effective, and probably the most common, technique used with children with anxiety disorders. The counselor will teach your child ways to think and behave differently to lessen the anxiety. Homework assignments are given to help your child practice the new skills in between sessions. Many of the suggestions in this book are based on this approach.

Counseling may last weeks or months depending on how severe the problem is. Ask your child's therapist for regular feedback to make sure progress is occurring. If you don't see progress, ask the therapist for an explanation.

## Will Medication Be Necessary?

When counseling is not working, or when the symptoms are so severe they're interfering with daily life, the therapist may recommend medication. Usually, a child psychiatrist will be consulted who can prescribe and monitor the medication. A child psychiatrist is a medical doctor with specialized training in working with children who are experiencing emotional and behavioral problems.

Before your child is placed on any medication, it's wise to insist on a full medical checkup complete with blood work. This way, the doctor can monitor any effects the medicine may have. Bring your child in for regular checkups once a medication has been prescribed.

While medicines can be very effective and safe when properly monitored, there can be risks. Ask the doctor or pharmacist about any concerns you have regarding safety, side effects, or other questions.

## A Special Note to Dads with Anxious Sons

Because men are often raised believing they have to be strong and overcome their fears without help, it's not unusual for a father to have trouble accepting his son's problems with anxiety. As a father, you may have trouble relating to your son's fears if you don't have problems with fears yourself. Or if you were fearful as a child, you may overreact by pushing your son too much to face his fears because you don't want him to go through what you did. You may be afraid that your son is being "wimpy" and wonder if talking "tough" with him will help him overcome his fear. Unfortunately, this often makes fears and anxieties worse, and can actually cause problems later in life. Your support now can help prevent future problems. Rather than be critical, assume the role of a supportive coach with your son. In the long run, you'll find that this works much better.

## Remember . . .

While it's hard to see your child struggle with worries and fears, you can provide valuable help. By monitoring your own behavior, helping your child learn and practice the exercises in this book, and pursuing counseling and medication when needed, you can help ensure that your child is able to overcome troubling fears and lead a more productive life.

## Other Resources and References

Barlow, D.H. *Anxiety and Its Disorders* (New York: The Guilford Press, 2002).

Bourne, E. J. *The Anxiety & Phobia Workbook* (Oakland, CA: New Harbinger Publications, Inc., 2000).

Coryell, W. & Winokur, G. *The Clinical Management of Anxiety Disorders* (New York: Oxford University Press, 1991).

*Diagnostic and Statistical Manual of Mental Disorders,* Fourth Edition (Washington, DC: American Psychiatric Association, 1994).

Foa, E. B. & Wilson, R. *Stop Obsessing!* (New York: Bantam Books, 2001).

Goleman, D. *Emotional Intelligence* (New York: Bantam Books, 1995).

Henricks, G. & Wills, R. *The Centering Book* (Englewood Cliffs, NJ: Prentice-Hall, 1975).

Hunt, D. *No More Fears* (New York: Warner Books, Inc, 1988).

Manaissas, K. *Keys to Parenting Your Anxious Child* (Hauppauge, NY: Barron's Educational Series, 1996).

Markway, B.G., Carmin, C.N., Pollard, C.A., & Flynn, T. *Dying of Embarrassment: Help for Social Anxiety and Phobia* (Oakland, CA: New Harbinger Publications, Inc., 1992).

Marsh, J.S. & Mulle, K. *OCD in Children and Adolescents* (New York: The Guilford Press, 1998).

Oaklander, V. *Windows to Our Children* (Highland, NY: The Center for Gestalt Development, Inc., 1988).

"Obsessive Compulsive Disorder: The Secret Childhood Epidemic," *The Child Therapy News* (King of Prussia, PA: The Center for Applied Psychology, Vol. 1, No. 2, December 1993).

Peurifoy, R. Z. *Overcoming Anxiety* (New York: Henry Holt and Company, 1997).

Rozman, D. *Meditating with Children* (Boulder Creek, CA: University of the Trees Press, 1975).

Schab, L.M. *The Coping Skills Workbook* (King of Prussia, PA: Childswork/Childsplay, 1996).

Scott, L.B. & Thompson, J. J. *Talking Time* (St. Louis, MO: Webster, 1951).

Sleek, S. "After the storm, children play out fears," *Monitor* (June 1998).

## Organizations

American Academy of Child and Adolescent Psychiatry
(202) 966-7300
*www.aacap.org*

American Psychiatric Association
703-907-7300
*www.psych.org*

American Psychological Association
1-800-374-2721
*www.apa.org*

Anxiety Disorders Association of America
(240) 485 -1001
*www.adaa.org*

Mental Health America
1-800-969-6642
*www.nmha.org*

National Alliance for the Mentally Ill
1-800-950-6264
*www.nami.org*

National Institute of Mental Health (NIMH)
1-866-615-6464
*www.nimh.nih.gov*

Obsessive Compulsive Foundation
(203) 401-2070
*www.ocfoundation.org*

# Index

# About the Author

**James J. Crist, Ph.D., CSAC,** is the clinical director and a staff psychologist at the Child and Family Counseling Center in Woodbridge, Virginia. He works with a wide variety of clients, including children, adolescents, adults, couples, and families. He specializes in working with attention disorders, depression, bipolar disorder, anxiety disorders, and drug and alcohol abuse. He is also an adjunct faculty member in the professional counseling program at Argosy University. Dr. Crist is a graduate of Williams College in Massachusetts and the University of North Carolina at Chapel Hill, where he earned his Ph.D. in clinical psychology. This is his fourth book.

# Other Great Books from Free Spirit

### What to Do When You're Sad & Lonely
A Guide for Kids
*by James J. Crist, Ph.D.*
This reassuring book offers strategies kids can use to beat the blues, get a handle on their feelings, make and keep friends, and enjoy their time alone. It also focuses on depression, bipolar disorder, grief, and other problems too big for kids to handle on their own, and describes what it's like to go to counseling. For ages 9–13.
*$9.95; 128 pp.; softcover; two-color illust.; 5⅜" x 8⅜"*

### What to Do When Good Enough Isn't Good Enough
The Real Deal on Perfectionism: A Guide for Kids
*by Thomas S. Greenspon, Ph.D.*
This book helps kids understand what perfectionism is, how it hurts them, and how to free themselves. Throughout, kids are encouraged to work with their parents or other adults to learn where their perfectionism comes from and ultimately how to accept themselves as they are. For ages 9–13.
*$9.95; 144 pp.; softcover; two-color illust.; 5⅜" x 8⅜"*

### Stress Can Really Get on Your NERVES!
*by Trevor Romain and Elizabeth Verdick*
More kids than ever feel worried, stressed out, and anxious every day. This book is a helping hand: reassuring words, silly jokes, and light-hearted cartoons let kids know they're not the only worry-warts on the planet—and they can learn to manage their stress. For ages 8–13.
*$8.95; 104 pp.; softcover; illust.; 5⅛" x 7"*

### The Doggy Dung Disaster & Other True Stories
Regular Kids Doing Heroic Things Around the World
*by Garth Sundem*
Thirty true stories profile kids around the world who used their heads, hearts, courage, and creativity to do great things—inspiring young readers to do the same. For ages 9–13.
*$9.95; 176 pp.; softcover; illust.; 5¼" x 7½"*

*To place an order or to request a free catalog of SELF-HELP FOR KIDS®
and SELF-HELP FOR TEENS® materials, please write, call, email, or visit our Web site*

**Free Spirit Publishing Inc.**
**217 Fifth Avenue North • Suite 200 • Minneapolis, MN 55401**
**toll-free 800.735.7323 • local 612.338.2068**
**fax 612.337.5050 • help4kids@freespirit.com • www.freespirit.com**